About the Author

Beth Olshansky has a B.F.A. in art from Clark University (Worcester, MA.) and a M.A.L.S. in Art/Dance/Movement from Wesleyan University (Middletown, CT.) in conjunction with The Institute for Movement Exploration. While her work with children and art spans two decades, Ms. Olshansky's keen interest in the creative process has led her to explore parallel processes in other art forms.

Ms. Olshansky presently teaches art and spontaneous movement forms to children and adults, in addition to her work with teachers. Her continued commitment to creative process has led her to develop her own art form within the field of improvisational dance.

Ms. Olshansky lives in New Hampshire with her husband and three daughters.

Acknowledgments

Special thanks to

- Noele Clews, who provided inspiration in the beginning;
- Emily Barkin, who painstakingly rewrote my text;
- Meg Gilman, who worked meticulously on the photographs;
- all the young artists who shared their enthusiasm and their art.

Dedication

To my mother, Helen Olshansky, who passed on her love of art to me, and to my three daughters, Misa, Shana, and Noami, for whom I hope to do the same.

About This Book

Fifteen years ago, I had the good fortune to become artist-in-residence at a private preschool in Portsmouth, New Hampshire. My five-year residency marked a time of intense learning for both the children and me. From the children, I relearned what is most basic to making art: the ability to play, dabble, and explore freely without expectation. I learned that young children, being masters of play, are natural artists. However, like adults, children work best in an environment that supports their artistic growth. So I learned how to create a working art environment for the youngest of artists. From me, the children learned tangible skills: how to watercolor, how to batik, how to make prints. More important, every child learned that he or she is an artist.

Portfolio of Illustrated Step-by-Step Art Projects for Young Children is an outgrowth of those years and the years that followed. While the activities were inspired by work with preschool artists, it has since grown to include artists through the elementary grades. It is a sharing of methods, project ideas, art work, and experiences.

There are few books on the market about working with the youngest of artists. Those that do exist tend to demean the child's artistic worth. What they tell the reader is that a young child's early art education must be frittered away making milk carton constructions until he or she is old enough to do "real art." This book fills a need; it presents real artistic challenges to young artists.

This book also shares a refreshing and highly successful approach to working with preschool and elementary children. Children are natural artists, and their processes and work must be treated with the utmost respect. This means presenting children with real artistic challenges that foster real artistic growth; providing them with high-quality tools and materials that are worthy of their efforts; respecting their process and allowing it to develop its own natural progression;

and mounting and displaying their work with care and pride.

Portfolio of Illustrated Step-by-Step Art Projects for Young Children is divided into three sections: Section One, "Creating the Art Environment," guides you through gathering supplies, designing the work space, setting up projects, adapting the projects to meet children's individual needs, cleaning up, and mounting the art work; Section Two, "The Progression of Art Experiences," describes the natural progression of artistic experience which is integral to the creative process. Once this progression is recognized and respected, it can be utilized to maximize a child's artistic growth. Section Three, "Step-by-Step Art Activities," offers just that—a collection of delightful projects in six different processes:

• DRAWING. Children begin with the flat two-dimensional plane and the simple line. Through a wide variety of materials, children explore line, what it can and cannot do, and how it can be used for abstraction or representation. Projects include "Chalk and Glue Drawing" and "Sgraffitto."

• PAINTING. Children are first introduced to the magical science of mixing colors through experimentation and trial-and-error. Children also become acquainted with a new tool—the paintbrush—and a new medium—paint. Projects include "Watercolor and Ink" and "Marbling."

• RESIST. A kind of magic takes hold as children become aware of their ability to create design through the use of resisting substances. Projects include "White Glue Resist" and "Batik."

• PRINTING. Children are offered two new options: either create an image through the use of found objects and stencils, or make a printing plate to reproduce an image repeatedly. For young artists who lack the fine-motor skills to work representationally, this offers them a fascinating way to play with design and imagery. For older children, it provides a way to repeat a favorite drawing or design. Projects include "Sponge Prints," "Etched Monoprints," and "Cardboard Shapes Relief Prints."

• COLLAGE AND RELIEF. These activities form a bridge between two- and three-dimensional art. Children now become aware of their option to create texture or build a design on top of a flat surface. As their pictures begin to bulge from the flat two-dimensional plane, design is explored and understood in a very physical, tactile way. Projects include "Tissue Collage Bird Hanging," "Eggshell Collage," and "Wooden Shapes Relief."

• SCULPTURE. Children are offered the very tactile experience of squeezing, twisting, rolling, and stretching materials between their fingers. These activities come easily to children as their natural desires to touch and feel take hold. Projects include "Clay: Slab Work," "Bread Dough Sculpture," and "Spool Puppet."

The projects and methods in *Portfolio of Illustrated Step-by-Step Art Projects for Young Children* have been designed, tested, redesigned, and retested. They work. Children of all ages should be repeatedly encouraged to follow the natural progression of art experiences, reinforcing and building upon newly acquired skills while constantly being stimulated and challenged. Natural rhythms of the creative process are thus utilized in designing the children's art experiences. You need only follow the simple step-by-step procedures and use common sense and respect for children in order to encourage the artist within each child to unfold!

Beth Olshansky

Many thanks to the following young artists whose works are featured in this book:

Jennifer Alley	Tamsen Garber	Greg Pike
Kristen Alley	Jason Godfrey	Kattie Place
Bekah Alvord	Rebecca Grishman	Jennifer Porter
Michelle Bakis	Matthew Hanfland	Hillary Prescott
Corinna Befort	Sarah Hoeksema	Heidi Rammer
Jenny Blair	Emily Howard	Andrew Ritzo
Robby Bogard	Kate Hubbard	Nathan Ritzo
Misa Brautigam	Alexis Johnson	Holly Rouleau
Shana Brautigam	Julie Kempton	Katy Savage
Elicia Carmichael	Robby Lamson	Pippa Schulman
Sarah Carmichael	Angela LePore	Gina Smith
Aaron Caswell	Daria Maneche	Christine Stilwell
The Children's Garden	Travis McKenzie	Summer Van Mullem
(Classes of '74, '77, '78)	Chris McQuarrie	Jimmy Wandmacher
Kimberly Coffey	Jen Mead	Meredith Watson
Kelly Coles	Gretchen Morehouse	Samantha Whitcomb
Shannon Connolly	Matthew Murphy	Michael Wimsatt
Beth Cottrell	Chris Nittle	Christy Wright
Gary Desjardins	Reena Patel	David Zwerg

Contents

SECTION THREE
STEP-BY-STEP ART ACTIVITIES • 11

Drawing • 11

Painting • 31

Resist • 62

Printing • 85

Section 1

Creating the Art Environment

When I first began working with young children and their art, I knew something about art and less about three- and four-year-olds. I did, however, suspect one thing to be true: Making art is in the same family as child's play and that children, being masters of play, would be natural artists. Naively, I trusted that all else would fall into place.

When I arrived at school, my hypothesis was challenged by a more basic issue—how to get the children out of their dress-ups and into the art room. Reams of manila paper and red and blue poster paints simply could not compete with wild hats, silk evening gowns, and old army jackets. It did not take me long to realize that in order for kids to create art, they first had to be enticed.

Agreeing with the children's preference for the imaginative and unusual, I began searching for ways to create an art environment that would not only stimulate young children, but would also consider their special needs. What follows here is the result of 15 years of working intensely with children of all ages: a list of steps that can be taken to create a working art environment for artists young and old.

GATHERING SUPPLIES

Finding materials. A wealth of materials can be gathered for next-to-nothing with a little ingenuity and some spare time. In our society of throw-aways and surplus, almost any business or industry has something to offer. Most retail shops, for example, have a variety of window display items which they regularly discard. Grocery stores abound with Styrofoam® and cardboard trays, and a variety of boxes. Ice cream parlors are great sources of round containers. Wallpaper stores give away old sample books. Fabric stores often donate scraps. Lumber mills are goldmines for scrap wood, sawdust, and wood chips. Rolls of newsprint can be purchased cheaply from your local press. Furniture stores and appliance dealers often have no further use for gigantic boxes. Neighbors, friends, and grandparents often have cellars and attics piled high with useful items.

Businesses are often more than happy to donate their surplus goods to a local school or enthusiastic parent, and a creative mind can find a use for almost anything. One of my best scavenges was a store mannequin which I found (naked and in pieces) in a department store alley on trash day. The kids went wild dressing it up with sequins and paint the next day.

Buying materials. Whatever materials cannot be found, can be purchased in bulk, at low cost, from school catalogues. These usually include the basics: reams of white paper, construction paper, glue, paint and paint brushes. Purchase only high quality materials; not only will they inspire more careful work on the part of the children, they will also produce more attractive and durable works of art. There is nothing as frustrating, for example, as finding hairs from an inexpensive paint brush spread across your carefully painted watercolor, or as discouraging as losing half of your collage pieces because of poor adhesive. Recycled computer paper may be fine for practicing name writing, but it is uninspiring when used for drawing pictures. Whatever is worth doing is worth doing well, and the materials should

reflect this. Using high quality tools and materials sets a standard of excellence for young artists. Children feel proud to be using fine materials and real artist's tools and they know that this privilege reflects your confidence in them as artists.

DESIGNING THE WORK SPACE

Walls. Walls should be painted white to create a sense of space and peace. White walls also provide a dignified background for displaying children's art work, similar to a gallery or museum.

Floors. Fear of making a mess can inhibit the creativity of a child. Therefore, make certain that floors are a type that can be easily cleaned. Polyurethane or linoleum surfaces are ideal. A stack of newspaper should also be available to cover the floor when a project requires it. An extremely messy project should be saved for a warm, sunny day and taken outdoors.

Windows. The art room should ideally contain large windows that provide natural lighting, ventilation when necessary, and a sense of open space.

Furniture. Sturdy, durable, appropriate-sized furniture is a must. In a school room, large tables that can accommodate several children working at once should be placed centrally in the art room. Smaller tables that can accommodate one or two children should be set in remote corners of the room to encourage individual work that requires sustained concentration. All furniture should be able to be easily cleaned; urethane surfaces or Formica® tabletops are recommended for this reason.

Wash place. The work area should contain a sink that

is easily accessible. If this is impossible, station a footstool near the sink, or provide a low washbasin near the work area.

Supply storage area. Two different storage areas for art supplies should be created: One area that is within reach of children and one that is out of reach. A low bookcase makes an ideal storage space for those suplies which children can safely help themselves to, such as paper, pencils, rulers, chalk, crayons, markers, clay, and round-tipped scissors. Out-of-reach shelves and cupboards should contain those supplies that require adult supervision or assistance to use.

Drying/storage area. Drying art work can be tacked onto bulletin boards, clothed-pinned to drying lines, or laid flat in out-of-the-way places. Cubbyholes make ideal compartments for storing completed works of art. A print drying rack is also a worthwhile investment as it allows for drying many pieces of art work in a small amount of space.

CONSIDERATIONS WHEN SETTING UP PROJECTS

Before beginning any project, ask yourself the following questions. (This is particularly important when working with very young artists.)

● How many children can work comfortably at one table? Over-crowding the work table creates confusion and results in frustration, unnecessary spills, and territorial fights. A fairly simple project such as watercolor painting is best accomplished at a large table that seats several children comfortably. Batik, on the other hand, is a more complex procedure and demands a work station at which only one or two children can work.

● What accidents can happen? Anticipate all possible accidents, then ask yourself how they can be avoided. For example, if you anticipate water spillage, be sure to use broad-based, heavy containers placed centrally on the table. This way, water is accessible to all, yet is removed from the edges of the table.

● Am I prepared for an accident? If a spill does occur, is the necessary equipment available to handle it? Sponges, paper towels, and art smocks should be standard equipment for any project.

ADAPTING PROJECT VARIABLES AND WORK RHYTHMS TO MEET CHILDREN'S NEEDS

Tailoring Project Variables to the Very Young

Art projects should be designed to accommodate the developmental strengths and limitations of young children. While children should be consistently challenged to develop new skills, project variables such as tool-size, paper-size, and procedures should always support the child's ability to meet these challenges. For example, if a child is asked to paint a large picture, provide a large piece of paper and a large paint brush. Never give a child a large piece of paper and a small brush and expect him/her to fill the paper with paint. The child's attention span simply will not allow it.

Be sensitive and responsive to children's fine motor and conceptual abilities as well as to their attention span. If a particular project or medium is new to a three- or four-year-old (a) introduce it in a gradual, systematic way so that the child is not overwhelmed by too many options; (b) work repeatedly so that the child can grasp the artistic concept as well as gain skill from working with the materials and processes over time; (c) select tools and paper that are of a size and shape that engage the child's dexterity but do not frustrate him or her; and (d) tailor tools and materials to the child's attention span so that the child is able to sustain interest and complete the project.

While the same guidelines hold true for older children, in general, older children can handle more project variables at once, grasp more complex processes, and make more directed choices based on a desired end result.

Responding to Individual Work Rhythms

All children have their own individual work rhythm, and should be encouraged to respond to their own varying needs on a daily basis. This is especially true of young children. One child, for example, may enjoy repeating the same project several times in one day or over a few days' time. Still another may become satiated doing one project early in the day and may want to become involved in a totally different activity in the afternoon. Each of these needs is valid and should be accommodated.

In order to accommodate a variety of personal needs in one classroom, set up the following situation each day (a) one major art project, centrally located, which is a focus for the day; and (b) several alternative projects located elsewhere in the art room which are available to those children who require a variety of experiences. Alternative projects should be those that children can accomplish without supervision such as clay sculpting, magic marker drawing, painting at the easel, or working on a favorite past project.

Building a Progression of Experience

The most effective way to acquaint a child with a particular medium is to encourage the child to work that medium over an extended period of time and in several different ways. A watercolor experience might, for example, last one to three weeks and could consist of the following sequence of events (a) a simple and precise lesson in basic watercolor technique; (b) exploring watercolor on dry paper; (c) exploring watercolor on wet paper; (d) exploring watercolor on rice paper or textured paper; (e) exploring the use of pen and ink with watercolor on dry, wet, or rice paper; (f) painting with watercolor and glue; and (g) painting with sand and glue, then watercolor to create a textured painting. Encouraging the child to participate in a series of related projects will increase the child's understanding of and comfort with the medium. It will also provide opportunities for the child to develop skills and ultimately master the medium, and most importantly, will inspire the child to add his/her own dimensions and flourishes to the work.

CLEANING UP

No child enjoys opening a jar of paint still muddied from last week's project, or using a stiff brush caked with old paint. Like adults, most children cannot create comfortably in a chaotic, cluttered, or messy work space. Kids take pride in being given the responsibility to care for their art supplies and keep their work space clean and orderly. In fact, clean-up fosters a sense of self-reliance and self-worth in the child. For these reasons, as well as economic ones, clean-up should be an "event" each day.

In group situations, clean-up provides an opportunity for children to work together as a team. Besides all this, clean-up can be plain old fun. I have vivid memories of color smeared, soapsudsed tabletops washed by soggy sponges and squealing children. The kid's enthusiasm for this daily ritual could not be squelched, even by the lure of snack time.

MOUNTING ART WORK

The following is a simple, inexpensive way to mount children's art work.

Select a mat. Select a piece of construction paper that is similar or identical in color to a particular feature in the picture that you wish to bring forward or accentuate. If a bold red circle is the focal point of a child's painting, then choose a red mat to frame it.

Trim the picture. Trim the work of art by removing all jagged edges, squaring the corners, and eliminating large areas of unused space (unless they are an integral part of the work).

Cut the mat. Cut the construction paper to a size proportionately larger than the picture. Generally, a one- or two-inch "frame" on all four sides is appropriate. Using a paper cutter will ensure a smooth, timesaving, and professional cutting job.

Affix the picture to the mat. Smear the back of the picture with rubber cement glue, paying particular attention to the corners and edges. Next, center the picture over the colored mat so that all four sides are equidistant from the edges of the mat. Press down on the picture to make it adhere to the mat.

Attach name tag. Make a small name tag with the artist's name neatly printed on it. Hang this tag on the wall beneath or beside the artist's work, gallery-style.

Mounting art work acknowledges a job well done and a fine product. It lets the children know that their work is special.

PRECAUTIONS WHEN USING HOT WAX

Hot wax is extremely flammable. Nevertheless, it can be used safely, even by young children, if the following precautions are taken.

- The safest, easiest method for melting wax is to place it in an unwanted electric frypan that has temperature settings on the dial. Remember
  - Wax will melt at 225° F.
  - Wax will begin to smoke at temperatures above 225° F. (A warning signal.)
  - Wax will burst into flames at 333° F.
- *Never melt wax at temperatures higher than 225° F.*
- Instruct children *never* to touch the hot wax or the frypan.
- Never leave children unsupervised.
- Set up the project in an out-of-the-way place.
- Make sure that electrical cords are out of the path of feet.
- Limit the number of children working at one time.
- Never melt wax in a pot that is placed directly on a flame or burner, as this can cause a wax fire.
- A wax fire can be put out with baking soda, so keep a large box handy. Never put water on a wax fire as this will cause a splattering of hot wax.
- Paraffin residue should never be ingested. Once a frypan has been used for melting wax, it should never be used for cooking again.

- Melt wax in a well-ventilated room—especially if wax is to be heated over several hours.
- Impress children with a sense of caution and responsibility when working with hot wax.
- Caution: With very young children, allow only one child at a time to work with hot wax in a closely supervised situation.

Section 2

The Progression of Art Experiences

A child's artistic growth can be maximized by the thoughtful ordering of art experiences. To do this, it is necessary to recognize that the creative process does not begin and end with individual art experiences, but rather forms an ongoing progression of experience that evolves over time. Thus, the skill children acquire, the understandings they gain, the imagery they create during one art experience are all carried into the next. Each subsequent experience builds upon the former experiences, embellishes them, or takes them in a new direction, as children push beyond their own limitations.

To foster this artistic growth, a natural progression of experiences should be presented to the child. Projects should be thoughtfully selected and introduced in the form of a series or progression in which the child works at a very basic level, then gradually builds upon his or her experience. Thus, if a child is to work in watercolor, a simple and precise lesson in basic watercolor technique should be given first. The child should be encouraged to explore this basic technique thoroughly and repeatedly. When the child has gained some skill and understanding of the process, she/he can move on to simple variations: watercolor on wet paper, for instance. With the introduction of each new variation, newly acquired skills are reinforced and the child continues to be challenged. The challenge remains manageable, however, for the child greets it with a strong foundation. In this way, the child learns quickly, meets new challenges comfortably, feels good about him or herself and his or her growing abilities, acquires confidence as well as skill, and is eager to take on new challenges. The child becomes highly-tuned emotionally and technically for the very best art experience.

This book is arranged to encourage a natural progression of experiences. While individual projects can be successfully worked in any order, for maximum growth it is recommended that the overall progression of this book be followed.

Give each child time with each new process, then allow the child to build upon the experience through a series of related yet varied experiences, working from simple to complex. When the child's interest begins to wane, it is time to move onto something new. Follow the general outline of this book where it feels right and seems appropriate. Create your own structure where you see fit. Above all, *listen to your children*. Let their needs ultimately guide you.

Notes on Michelle: A Progression of Experience

Michelle, age four, sits down to work with a pen and ink. I instruct her to wet her paper with a sponge and then draw on it, using any of the colored inks available that day.

She soaks her paper with the sponge and begins to draw on it with red ink, the brightest color. Michelle draws formlessly. To her surprise, the ink "explodes" as it meets the wet page. She watches and giggles, delighted.

Next, she tries the green and black inks, the other two color choices. Again she draws with the ink in a seemingly formless way. When she finishes her design, she begins to sign her name in black. As Michelle draws across a puddle of water, the letters of her name "explode like a volcano." She squeals.

Immediately, she grabs a second piece of paper and this time wets it a little less liberally. She chooses to draw with only the black ink—the same color that had captured her fancy a moment before. This time, a face emerges from the page. Having used drier paper and having become more adept with her bamboo pen, Michelle is able to depict an image more clearly.

Recognizing her intention to work representationally, I suggest to Michelle that she try a third picture on dry paper: an experiment. Using the same bamboo pen and black ink, Michelle works again with the image of a face. This time she is so pleased with the growing clarity of her image that she proudly signs her mother's name, Beth, to the page.

Michelle chooses to work one more time on dry paper. Her fourth and final picture is a lovely outgrowth of her previous three experiences. Having gained skill with her tool and understanding of her medium, she adds more detail to her representation. This picture again earns her mother's signature. It is clear that Michelle is pleased.

Michelle does not go on to do another picture. Having completed her progression of experience, she lays down her pen.

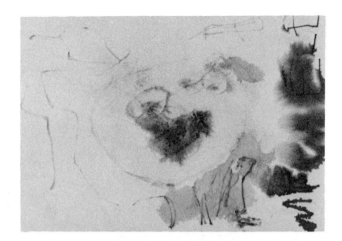

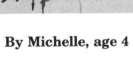

By Michelle, age 4

Section 3

Step-by-Step Art Activities

DRAWING

Shana, nine months old, plays outside on the large, granite doorstep in front of the house. She picks up a small white stone and begins to scrape it across the granite slab. Lines appear. She seems unsurprised, purposeful in her actions. She continues to scrape the stone. More lines appear. In this way, she makes her very first drawing.

At some point in their early lives, all children pick up a stone, a twig, a pencil, or a pinecone and begin to make marks. This experience may happen by accident, or it may occur as a result of imitation. Either way, children realize that they have the power to alter a surface, to create.

As a child's skill and understanding evolve, these early markings begin to acquire form. The child will gradually depict shapes, then images on paper. The child will draw his or her first circle and that circle will become an image of the sun. Later, the sun will become the child's own face. Later still, the sun's rays will become arms and legs radiating from the central sun-head. Through simple linear markings, the child enters the world of two-dimensional art.

In the next few activities the child explores the simple line. Through the use of many line-producing tools and media, the young artist will discover what lines can and cannot do; what kinds of tools and media produce particular kinds of lines; and how line can be used for abstraction or representation.

NOTES ON MATTHEW: A LESSON IN DRAWING

It is two days before Easter and Matthew, age 4, desperately wants to draw a picture of a bunny. Christian has brought a stuffed bunny to school. Matthew sees it and says, "I want to draw *that* bunny."

He places the bunny on a piece of paper and attempts to use it as a stencil. This does not work. Frustrated and forlorn, he asks me to draw the bunny for him. Instead I say, "Look at the bunny. What shape is its head? What shape is its body? Really look hard at the bunny, then draw it."

Matthew scrutinizes the bunny's form. He peers. He squints. Then slowly he puts his pencil to the paper and begins to outline the bunny's shape. His pencil jerks and quivers as he draws the roundness of the bunny's cheek. His line then climbs steadily upward as he depicts each curve in the bunny's head.

Matthew pauses to check his work, his eyes darting back and forth from drawing to bunny to drawing again. He begins once more, this time shooting a line upward over the mountain of one ear and then the other. Matthew's line slides quickly downward, along the other side of the bunny's face. He works diligently, his moments packed with concentration. With his careful line, Matthew caresses the bunny's shape.

When Matthew finishes outlining the bunny's body, his attention breaks. Perfunctorily, he adds eyes, a nose, four legs, and a nub of a tail. Then he lovingly colors the bunny a bright orange. When Matthew is done, he eyes his picture thoughtfully. A puzzled look appears on his face, as if something has gone wrong. But soon he breaks into a grin and shouts, "Look! I made a BUNNY- PIG!" Matthew jumps up out of his seat and marches over to the bulletin board to tack up his bunny-pig for all to see.

By Matthew, age 4

Activity 1 • Self-Portrait

Age Level: Preschool and up

Notes:

- At any age, self-portraits are a great record of developmental stage and self-concept.

- It can be fun as well as fascinating to have your child(ren) repeat this project several times throughout the year as a record of their personal growth.

- Self-portraits can mark the beginning of an entire unit on the child. Young children can make "All About Me" books that begin with a self-portrait and can include handprints, height, weight, a story about themselves, a drawing of a favorite toy or animal, a portrait of their family, an illustrated list of likes and dislikes, and so on.

- Large body tracings can be used to begin a study of the body: What's under the skin, or how the body works.

- Older children may want to explore the concept of self-portraits through a variety of materials, such as chalk drawing, watercolors, watercolor and ink, collage, clay modeling, papier-mâché masks, and papier-mâché puppets.

By Misa, age 6

Self-Portrait

MATERIALS
- Mirror
- White construction paper
- Markers

OPTIONAL
- Newsprint roll

1

Look in the mirror.

2

Look at the shapes and colors of your facial features. See where they are in relation to one another.

3

With a marker, draw the shape of your face.

4

Now with the appropriate colors, draw your facial features: eyes, nose, ears, mouth, hair.

5

Notice the details on your face. Do you have freckles? Are your eyelashes long?

6

Draw what you see.

7

Now on a bigger paper, draw your whole body, or have someone else trace your body on a large piece of paper while you are lying down. Color in your body features.

Activity 2 • Magic Pencils

Age Level: Preschool and up

NOTES: It is not often that one approach works for all children. This is one time when it did!

THE DAY OF THE MAGIC PENCILS

It is a gray day, and winter is beginning to feel like a way of life rather than a passing season. The children and I need something to revive our spirits.

I bring to school a new box of colored pencils that "paint" when they are dipped in water. I have used pencils similar to these at home, but today I find them particularly captivating. Before the children arrive, I slide into a tiny chair and begin to dabble. On the smooth, velveteen surface of my paper, images of many colors unfold before me and grow, as if they have a mind of their own. Despite my growing awareness that the children will soon be arriving, I cannot put these magic pencils down.

The children begin to arrive. They see me working at the art table and immediately come over to watch. I continue to work, pausing only now and then to answer questions. One little girl eyes my picture for awhile. She asks, "What are you making?" Quite honestly I reply, "I'm making a design." My absorption is compelling; a number of children join me at the table. We work together happily. Sometimes there is silence as we work, other times we chat about the pictures we are making. There is a special feeling about this experience. We are all artists working together in a medium we love.

By Elicia, age 7

Magic Pencils

MATERIALS
- White construction paper or white bristol paper
- Color pencils that "paint" when dipped in water*
- Paper towels
- Glass of water
- Watercolor brush

*These are special colored pencils available at art supply store.

1 Lay paper towel on table and place a small piece of white paper over it. The towel helps to absorb drips and keep paper and table clean.

2 Dip colored pencil in water.

3 Draw with it.

4 Use several colors, dipping each in water before using.

5 Make a line drawing or fill in areas with solid color.

6 VARIATION: Try using pencils dry and then brushing water over drawing when complete.

7 Do not leave pencils in water or they will dissolve.

Activity 3 • Chalk Drawing

Age Level: Preschool and up

Notes:

- Chalk can be used in combination with many other materials. (See Activity 4, "Chalk and Glue Drawings"; Activity 12, "Watercolor and Chalk"; and Activity 35, "Sponge Prints and Chalk.")

- Texture rubbings using the side surface of chalk may be done with chalk on many different surfaces to explore the idea of tactile as well as visual textures. Children can record several different textures on a single piece of paper with one or more colors of chalk, or they may record just one texture with several different colors, turning the paper at many different angles. Try cutting out texture-rubbing shapes and making a collage.

- Older children can first explore texture through a partner-led blindfold walk to reawaken their tactile senses before doing texture rubbings.

- A spray fixative may be used over chalk drawings to keep them from smudging. CAUTION: Spray fixative should be applied only by an adult in a well-ventilated room.

- Take colored chalk outside and do a huge sidewalk drawing or a giant mural.

By Robby, age 5

Chalk Drawing

MATERIALS
- White construction paper
- Colored construction paper
- Colored chalk

OPTIONAL
- Bowl of water
- Sponge
- Bowl of buttermilk or thick, powdered milk
- Textures. For example, corrugated cardboard, widemesh screen, rough lumber, etc.

1 Try drawing with chalk on dry paper.

2 Then wet a different paper with a sponge.

3 Draw on it. Notice the difference.

4 Now sponge buttermilk onto another piece of paper.

5 Draw on it. How is it different?

6 Try placing textures beneath your paper. Rub across the paper's surface with the side of a piece of chalk. Use lots of colors.

7 Find textures in the room to do rubbings of, or go to the nearest cemetery and do gravestone rubbings.

1603 — 1625

Activity 4 • Chalk and Glue Drawing
Age Level: Preschool and up

Notes:

- Success with this project depends upon allowing the glue to totally dry and also thoroughly coloring in each outlined area to create areas of bright color to contrast the black background.

- Older children can coordinate a theme idea with a background color such as a night scene on black paper or a jungle scene on green paper.

- For a slightly different effect, chalk may be dipped in buttermilk.

- An abstract design on a black background can give a stained-glass window effect.

By Misa, age 6

Chalk and Glue Drawing

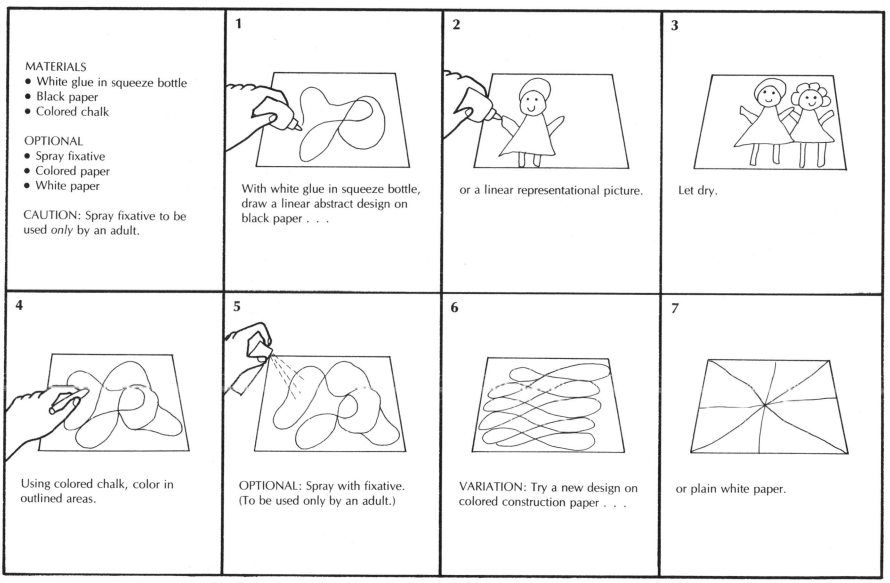

MATERIALS
- White glue in squeeze bottle
- Black paper
- Colored chalk

OPTIONAL
- Spray fixative
- Colored paper
- White paper

CAUTION: Spray fixative to be used *only* by an adult.

1 With white glue in squeeze bottle, draw a linear abstract design on black paper . . .

2 or a linear representational picture.

3 Let dry.

4 Using colored chalk, color in outlined areas.

5 OPTIONAL: Spray with fixative. (To be used only by an adult.)

6 VARIATION: Try a new design on colored construction paper . . .

7 or plain white paper.

Activity 5 • Pen and Ink

Age Level: First grade and up

Notes:

- Smocks should be worn to protect children's clothing. Take care to set up this project in a "spillproof" fashion. Ink should be placed within easy reach at the center of the table.
- Ink drawing may be combined with other materials. For example, watercolor and ink on wet paper make lovely note cards.

- Older children may want to do an ink drawing and then fill it in with watercolors once it is dry. This technique can create wonderful landscapes, still lifes, or self-portraits.
- The bamboo pens used in this activity are inexpensive and may be purchased at an art supply store.

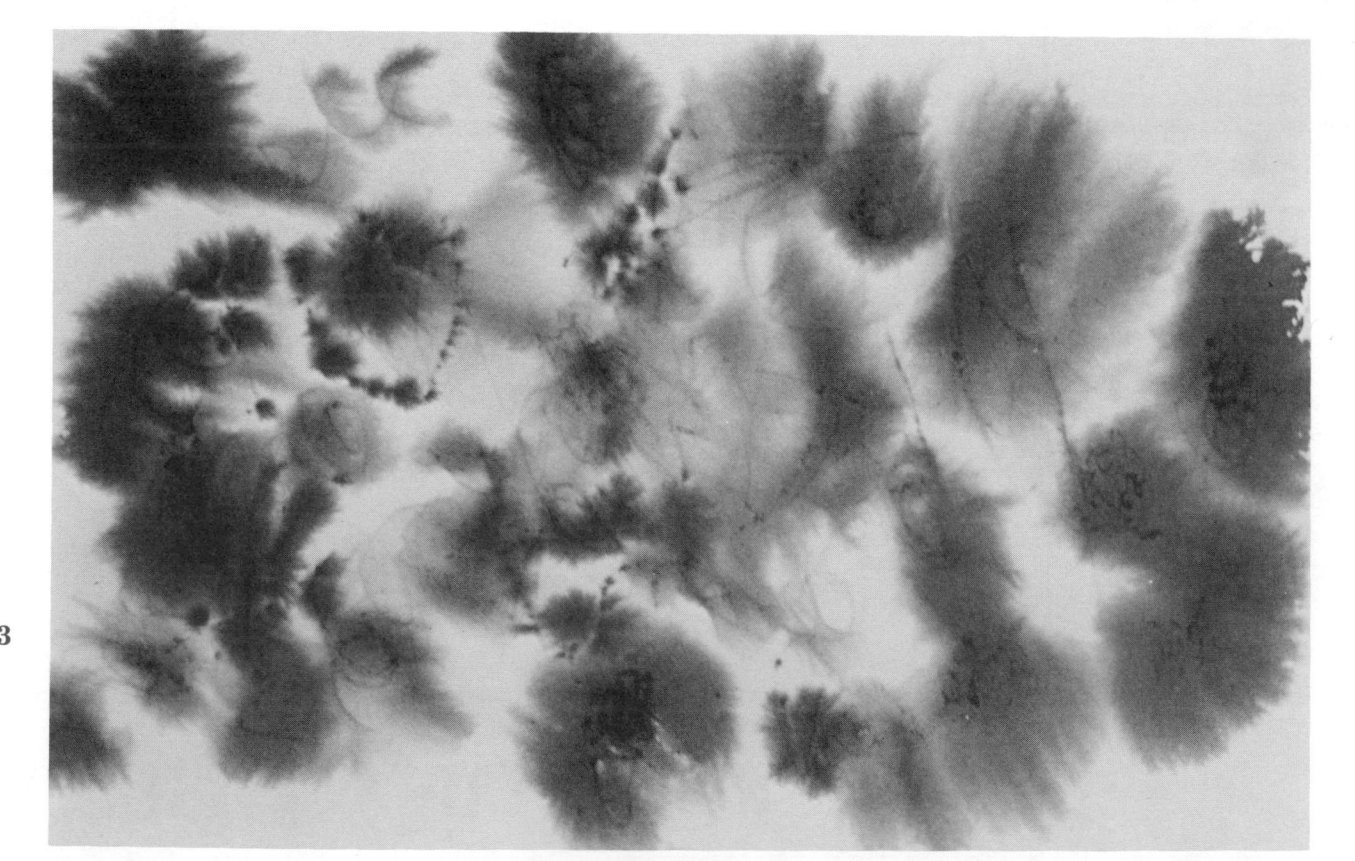

By Michael, age 3

Pen and Ink

MATERIALS
- White construction paper or Bristol paper
- Black and/or colored ink
- Bamboo pen or dried-up, felt-tipped pens
- Bowl of water
- Sponge

OPTIONAL
- Blotter paper
- A variety of papers

1 Set one bamboo or felt-tipped pen in each color of ink. Try using both types of pens or ink bottle squeeze-top as drawing tools.

2 Thoroughly moisten paper's surface with wet sponge.

3 With ink(s), draw a design or picture on paper.

4 Watch ink "explode" as it spreads and runs across wet paper surface.

5 VARIATION: Try using ink on dry paper. Note the difference.

6 VARIATION: Draw with ink on blotter paper. Watch ink spread in a different way.

7 Try drawing with ink on a variety of different papers. See what happens.

Activity 6 • Sgraffitto

Age Level: First grade and up

Notes:

- Smocks should be worn to protect children's clothing.
- A small amount of liquid soap may be added to the ink instead of glue to keep the ink adhering to crayon. Try out both methods and see which one works better for you.

- For an easier scratchboard technique for younger children, see Activity 7, "Plaster Scratchboard."
- Take care to set up ink in a spillproof fashion, placing the ink mixture in a low, wide-based container in the center of the table.

By Kelly, age 9

Sgraffitto

MATERIALS
- Oaktag, heavy untextured paper, or white-shirt cardboard cut into approx. 5"×7" pieces
- Crayons
- Black ink
- White glue
- Watercolor or sponge brushes (1")
- Empty margarine tub
- Pointed toothpicks

1

Mix together a small amount of white glue and black ink in a margarine tube. (Just enough glue so that ink will adhere to crayon surface.)

2

Bearing down hard with crayons, color entire paper with a thick layer of crayon. Use many bright colors.

3

With sponge brush or paint brush, coat picture evenly with ink-glue solution.

4

Let dry, approximately 5–15 minutes.

5

With pointed toothpick or other pointed object, scratch a design onto black surface.

6

Draw lines with toothpick, or make shapes of color by scratching out large areas of black ink.

7

POINTERS:
1) It is essential that every bit of white paper is covered with crayon in order for scratches to show brightly.
2) If too much glue is used, ink may not sufficiently scratch away. Try a less gluey solution.

Activity 7 • Plaster Scratchboard

Age Level: Preschool and up

Notes:

- This scratchboard technique is fun to make and easy for preschoolers to do. Older children can create quite elaborate detailed pictures or designs.
- Children should wear smocks to protect their clothing.
- Working with plaster of paris can be intriguing. Try doing several different plaster of paris projects so that children can become familiar with this unusual material. (See Activity 23, "Fresco.")

- Since plaster dries quickly, make sure you have all the necessary materials and equipment handy *before* you begin mixing the plaster.

- Place the ink in a spillproof, wide-based container at the center of the table.

By Aaron, age 4

Plaster Scratchboard

MATERIALS
- Styrofoam® or cardboard fruit or meat trays
- Plaster of paris
- Large bowl
- Wooden spoon
- Pitcher of water
- Water-soluble black ink
- Empty margarine tub for ink
- Paint or sponge brush
- Nail or sharp object (make certain nails are rust-free)

OPTIONAL
- Diluted food coloring

1
Mix plaster of paris and water according to directions on package. Stir quickly to dissolve plaster.

2
Quickly pour plaster into cardboard or Styrofoam® tray.

3
If plaster is thick, shake to level surface.

4
When plaster hardens, brush ink on plaster to cover the entire surface.

5
When ink is dry, scratch a design in plaster with a nail or sharp object.

CAUTION: Do not leave children unsupervised when using nails.

6
VARIATIONS: Try painting plaster surface with diluted food coloring first and then when dry, ink over with black ink. When surface is then scratched, lines will be colored . . .

7
or try painting food coloring over a heavily scratched surface and then rescratching. This will also add color to the board.

Activity 8 • Stained-Glass Drawing

Age Level: Preschool and up

Notes:

- Older children can create stained-glass designs using their name as a basis instead. (See Activity 10, "Stained-Glass Name Paintings.")

- These drawings make particularly nice cards and decorations around the winter holidays.

- These stained-glass pictures can also be created with tissue paper laid on top of a marker drawing and glued down with a wash of white glue and water. (See Activity 51, "Tissue Collage.")

- Modge-Podge® or other glossy finish may be purchased at an art store or craft shop.

By Misa, age 6

Stained-Glass Drawing

MATERIALS
- White paper
- Scissors
- Permanent markers, black & other colors
- Rubber cement
- Black construction paper
- Modge-Podge® or other glossy finish
- Sponge brush
- Paper for mounting

CAUTION: Rubber cement should be used *only* under close adult supervision.

1

Cut an arch shape out of white paper.

2

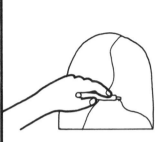

With black marker draw a design of curved or straight lines.

3

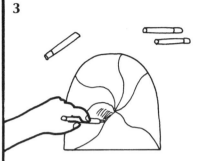

Color in shapes with colored markers.

4

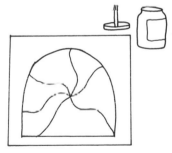

With rubber cement, glue drawing onto black construction paper.

5

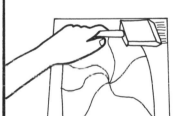

Apply glossy finish with sponge brush.

6

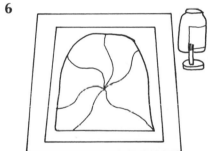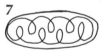

When dry, glue onto appropriate backing.

7

Try several different shapes for windows. Mount them as cards or hang them on your wall.

PAINTING

From the simple line, the young artist now moves on to a new medium, paint, and a new tool, the paintbrush. Solid areas of color are now within the child's reach as are a wide range of possibilities in visual texture and shading. The young artist delights in a newly discovered power: the ability to create new colors by mixing two or more existing colors together. To the inexperienced painter, this process falls within the realm of magic and is worthy of some focused attention. Moreover, as the simplest scratching of a single line was once a source of fascination, so now the stroking of the brush, the caressing of the page, the mixing and spreading of color are all new and captivating.

In the painting activities and in the next group of activities using resist, many of the projects involve the use of watercolors in combination with other media. It is essential that children be taught the proper use and care of watercolors and be given ample opportunity to explore basic watercolor technique before going on to more complex variations such as watercolor and ink or sand painting. With the introduction of each new process, it is important that children be given time to fully explore the possibilities and limitations of each new medium. For the young artist, the process of creating is the central artistic experience, and the product is merely the result of that experience.

MISA'S FIRST WORKS: PROCESS VERSUS PRODUCT

Misa, age three, takes great delight in making "watercolors" which consist of a faint muddy wash of paint spread across her paper. I have instructed her several times in the proper use of watercolors, but she seems unable to catch on. I surrender and let her play.

One day I look over to see her painting with bright clean colors. I become very excited, "Misa, what lovely bright colors you're making! I see purple and red, and there's a spot of green." Misa laughs, obviously delighted. "You must have remembered to wash your brush." She nods proudly. "Would you like to do another painting?" I ask. "Yup!" she squeals.

Enthusiastically, I replace Misa's painting with a clean sheet of paper, carefully setting aside her art work. Misa applies bright clean colors to her page. Again, I praise her painting technique; and again I carefully set aside her work, already having visions of matting and framing these first watercolors. Misa paints on, pleased with her pictures. I leave the area, not wanting to cramp her style with my overzealous watching.

Moments later, I return to find her busily working, babbling and singing, as she systematically stuffs each one of her lovely watercolors into the container of dirty wash water and proceeds to "wash" them as if she were doing her laundry. "Look," she calls out gaily, "washing!"

Activity 9 • Tempera Painting
Age Level: Preschool and up

Notes:

- In introducing tempera painting to young artists, it is important to begin simply with one and then two colors. Attention can thus be focused on applying the paint and returning the brush to the proper container. Once this has been mastered, colors may be changed and/or new colors added.

- Choose colors carefully, as young children tend to blend colors together. Try to avoid colors that will, in combination, easily muddy, such as red and green.

- Color-mixing is a whole science in itself and should definitely be explored by artists of all ages. There is a special satisfaction that comes with discovering and using new colors. Give children primary colors first. Give them a paper "palette" for exploring and mixing their own colors.

- A note about easels: Easels work well with thick, non-dripping paint. Otherwise, working on a flat surface is preferable.

- For preschoolers, spillproof containers are suggested.

- For young artists new to painting, large brushes work well. As more skill develops, smaller brushes may be substituted.

- Remember, as with introducing any new medium, process rather than product is of most importance.

By Emily, page 9

Tempera Painting

MATERIALS
- Large white paper
- Tempera paint in containers
- Large brushes
- Palette or tray

1 Set out 1 or 2 colors of paint, putting a brush in each container.

2 On large paper, apply paint, returning brush to proper container.

3 Add new color choices once 1 or 2 colors seems manageable.

4 To mix colors: Supply extra brushes and mixing palette or tray. Set out primary colors with a brush in each container.

5 On mixing palette, experiment with mixing colors together to create new colors. Use clean brush to actually blend new color.

6 Using new colors, paint a picture!

7 Try adding white to new colors to create pastel colors.

Activity 10 • Stained-Glass Name Painting

Age Level: Second grade and up

Notes:

- This project could be done as a class, using a long roll of newsprint paper (held vertically or horizontally) and having each child responsible for designing a specific area.

- This project can also be done with a variety of other materials including watercolor, watercolor and ink, watercolor and chalk, watercolor and glue, watercolor and crayon, and chalk and glue.

By Gary, age 10

Stained-Glass Name Painting

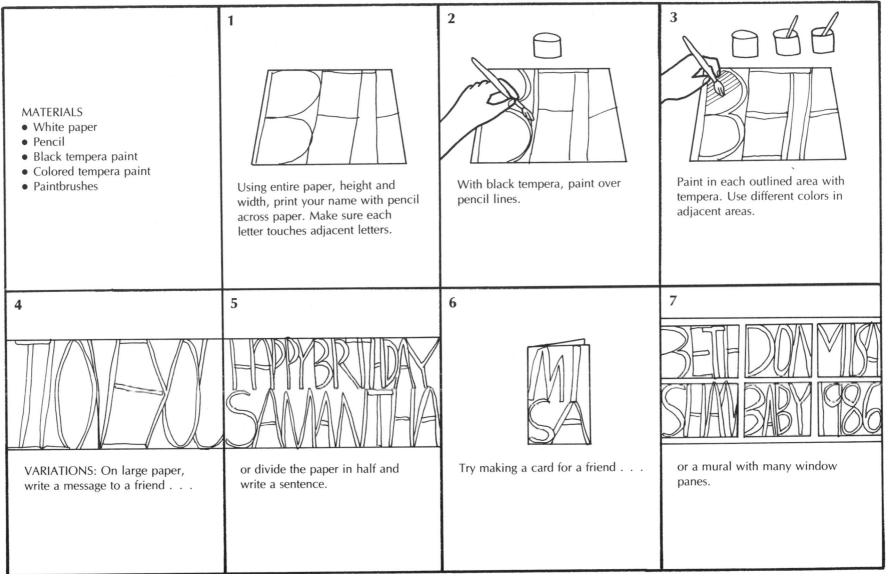

MATERIALS
- White paper
- Pencil
- Black tempera paint
- Colored tempera paint
- Paintbrushes

1 Using entire paper, height and width, print your name with pencil across paper. Make sure each letter touches adjacent letters.

2 With black tempera, paint over pencil lines.

3 Paint in each outlined area with tempera. Use different colors in adjacent areas.

4 VARIATIONS: On large paper, write a message to a friend . . .

5 or divide the paper in half and write a sentence.

6 Try making a card for a friend . . .

7 or a mural with many window panes.

Activity 11 • Watercolor

Age Level: Preschool and up

Notes:

DANIELLE

Danielle is a withdrawn, reluctant four year old. She spends her first few weeks of school "corner-hopping," watching other children play. She is unwilling to participate in any art projects, even upon special invitation. I have given up trying to encourage her to join us and for lack of a better alternative, I allow her to continue watching without being accosted by repeated invitations. Danielle continues to stand in corners.

One day a new box of watercolors catches Danielle's fancy. When no one is looking, she slides into a chair and quietly tries out the paints. She immediately becomes intrigued by the bright colors and absorbed in her own creations. Danielle makes two lovely water colors that day. It is clear that she is pleased.

The following day, Danielle sits down to work once more, though again she waits until no one is looking. The day after that, she begins to paint before school has even begun. Her paintings are special. Danielle knows this.

Days later, Danielle comes up to me, shy yet bright-eyed. She tugs on my clothing and points to her new t-shirt. It has on it a picture of an artist's palette and paint brush. "Look," she proudly proclaims, "I am an artist!" Danielle giggles, then skips off to take her place at the art table.

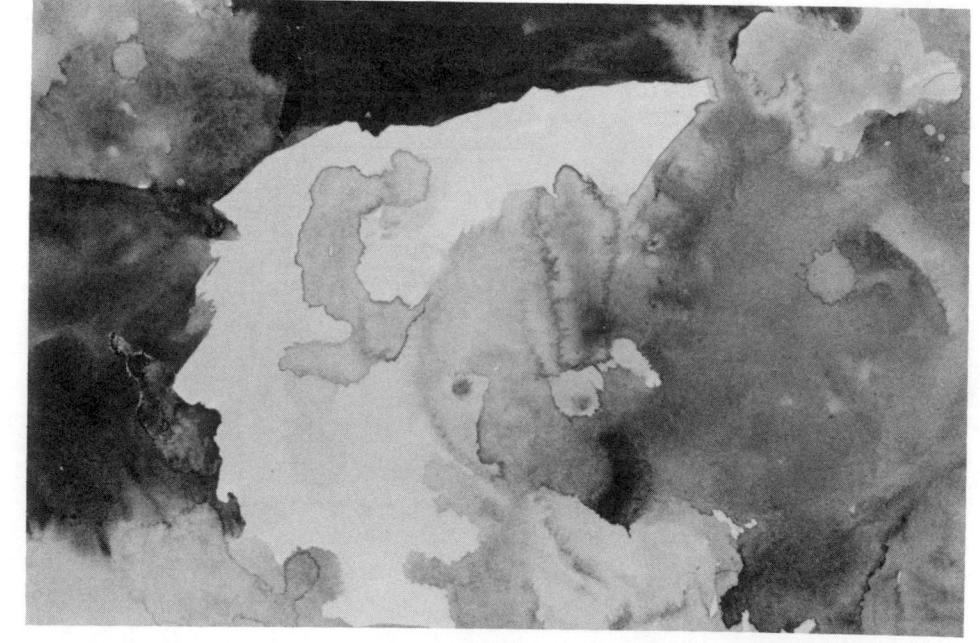

By Christy, age 3

Watercolor

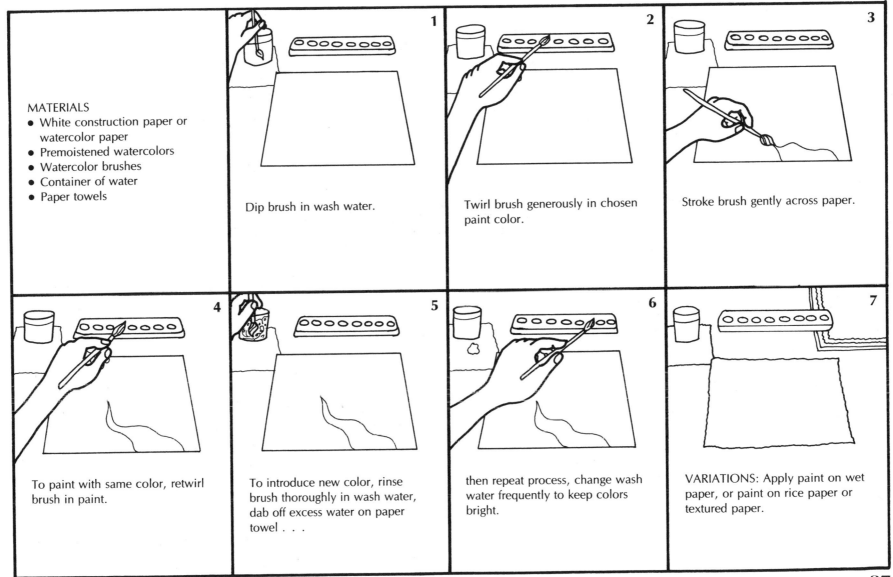

MATERIALS
- White construction paper or watercolor paper
- Premoistened watercolors
- Watercolor brushes
- Container of water
- Paper towels

1 Dip brush in wash water.

2 Twirl brush generously in chosen paint color.

3 Stroke brush gently across paper.

4 To paint with same color, retwirl brush in paint.

5 To introduce new color, rinse brush thoroughly in wash water, dab off excess water on paper towel . . .

6 then repeat process, change wash water frequently to keep colors bright.

7 VARIATIONS: Apply paint on wet paper, or paint on rice paper or textured paper.

Activity 12 • Watercolor and Chalk
Age Level: Preschool and up

Notes:

- This project can be extended by using watercolor and chalk in combination with any number of other painting and resist techniques: Sandpainting (Activity 16), Crayon Resist (Activity 24), Cray-Pas® Resist (Activity 25), White Glue Resist (Activity 26).

- For older children, mixed media offers a wonderful world of exploration.

By Aaron, age 4

Watercolor and Chalk

MATERIALS
- White construction paper
- Watercolors
- Watercolor brushes
- Glass of water
- Paper towels
- Colored chalk or pastels

OPTIONAL
- Sponge
- Buttermilk
- Charcoal sticks
- Colored construction paper
- Spray fixative

CAUTION: Spray fixative to be used *only* by an adult in a well-ventilated room.

1

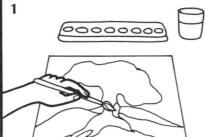

Paint a picture or design on paper with watercolors.

2

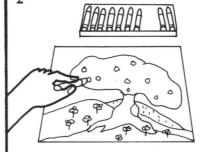

While paint is still wet, draw over it with colored chalks.

3

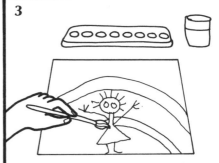

VARIATION 1: Draw with chalk on paper first, then paint over it with watercolors.

4

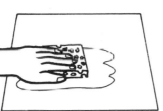

VARIATION 2: Try using chalk on white or colored paper which has been wet first with water or buttermilk.

5

VARIATION 3: Try using chalk and crayon together before or after using paint.

6

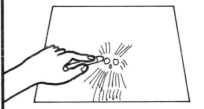

VARIATION: 4: Experiment with charcoals in the same way, before and after using paint.

7

Have an adult spray finish on picture to keep it from smudging.

Activity 13 • Rice Paper Painting
Age Level: Preschool and up

Notes:

- Rice paper paintings can make very delicate and beautiful pictures. Have children try out different kinds of rice paper.
- Small rice paper painting glued onto folded paper with rubber cement make lovely cards.

- Children should wear smocks to protect their clothing.
- CAUTION: If shellac or varnish is used, this should *only* be applied in a well-ventilated room by an adult.

By Summer, age 4

Rice Paper Painting

MATERIALS
- Inexpensive rice paper
- Manila paper
- Food coloring
- 4 baby food jars
- 4 brushes
- Water

OPTIONAL
- Black ink
- Thin felt-tipped pen
- Varnish or shellac
- Sponge brush
- Rubber cement glue

1

Dilute food coloring to desired shade in each jar. Place brush in each jar.

2

Place rice paper on top of manila paper to prevent wet rice paper from tearing when handled.

3

Paint food coloring on rice paper.

4

Always return brush to appropriate jar. Try filling the entire paper with color.

5

OPTIONAL STEP: While paper is still wet, dip thin felt-tipped pen into black ink. Outline colored designs or draw a new design on top of the painting.

6

VARIATIONS: Try waiting until paper is dry to draw with ink, or tear painted sheets of dry rice paper into pieces and make a collage.

7

Completed pictures can be coated with varnish or shellac for a hard, shiny surface.

CAUTION: This step to be done *only* by an adult.

Activity 14 • Splatter Painting

Age Level: Preschool and up

Notes:

- This project is messy so smocks should be worn to protect clothing.
- Give children a chance to do many splatter paintings so they have the opportunity to develop their "technique."
- Try having children splatter paint to various types of music. How do different musical pieces affect their paintings?
- For a very "moving" experience (and potentially quite messy), set up a roll of newsprint along a wall for a mural. Do this outside or with an abundance of newspaper on the surrounding area.
- When dry, splatter paintings can be cut and pasted to create a collage. Other types of paper, such as tissue or rice, may be used as well.

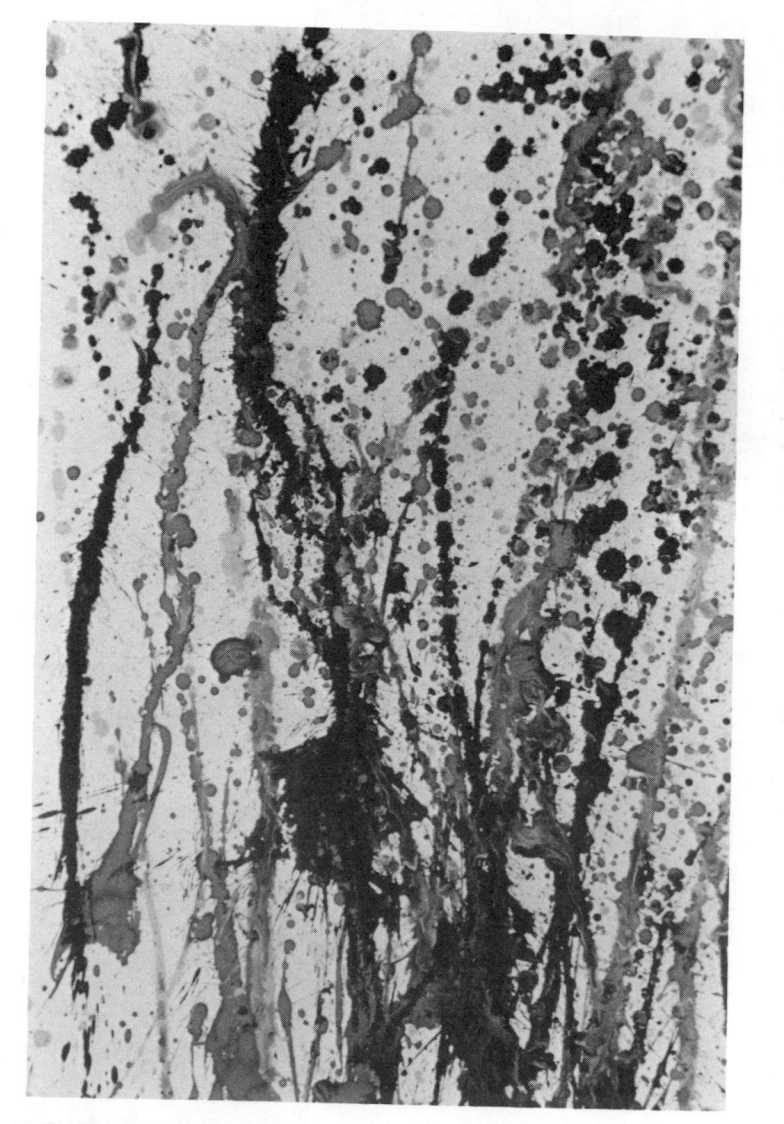

By Julie, age 6

Splatter Painting

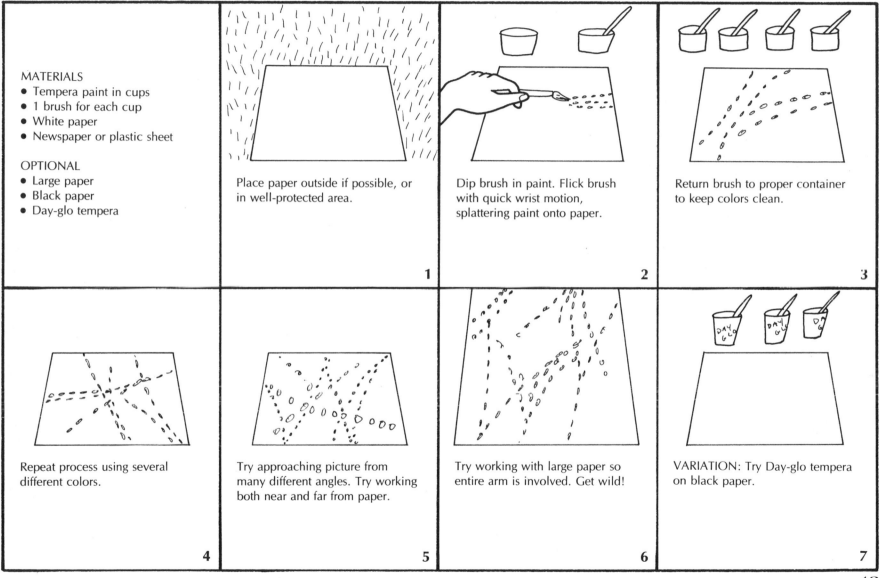

MATERIALS
- Tempera paint in cups
- 1 brush for each cup
- White paper
- Newspaper or plastic sheet

OPTIONAL
- Large paper
- Black paper
- Day-glo tempera

1 Place paper outside if possible, or in well-protected area.

2 Dip brush in paint. Flick brush with quick wrist motion, splattering paint onto paper.

3 Return brush to proper container to keep colors clean.

4 Repeat process using several different colors.

5 Try approaching picture from many different angles. Try working both near and far from paper.

6 Try working with large paper so entire arm is involved. Get wild!

7 VARIATION: Try Day-glo tempera on black paper.

43

Activity 15 • String Painting

Age Level: Preschool and up

Notes:

- Try string painting on colored paper.
- For a variation in design technique, have children try drawing string out from pressed paper after laying a paper on top of the string and pressing with the hand.

- Try adding a watercolor wash to string painting once it has dried. Have children follow the design of the string with the watercolor wash.

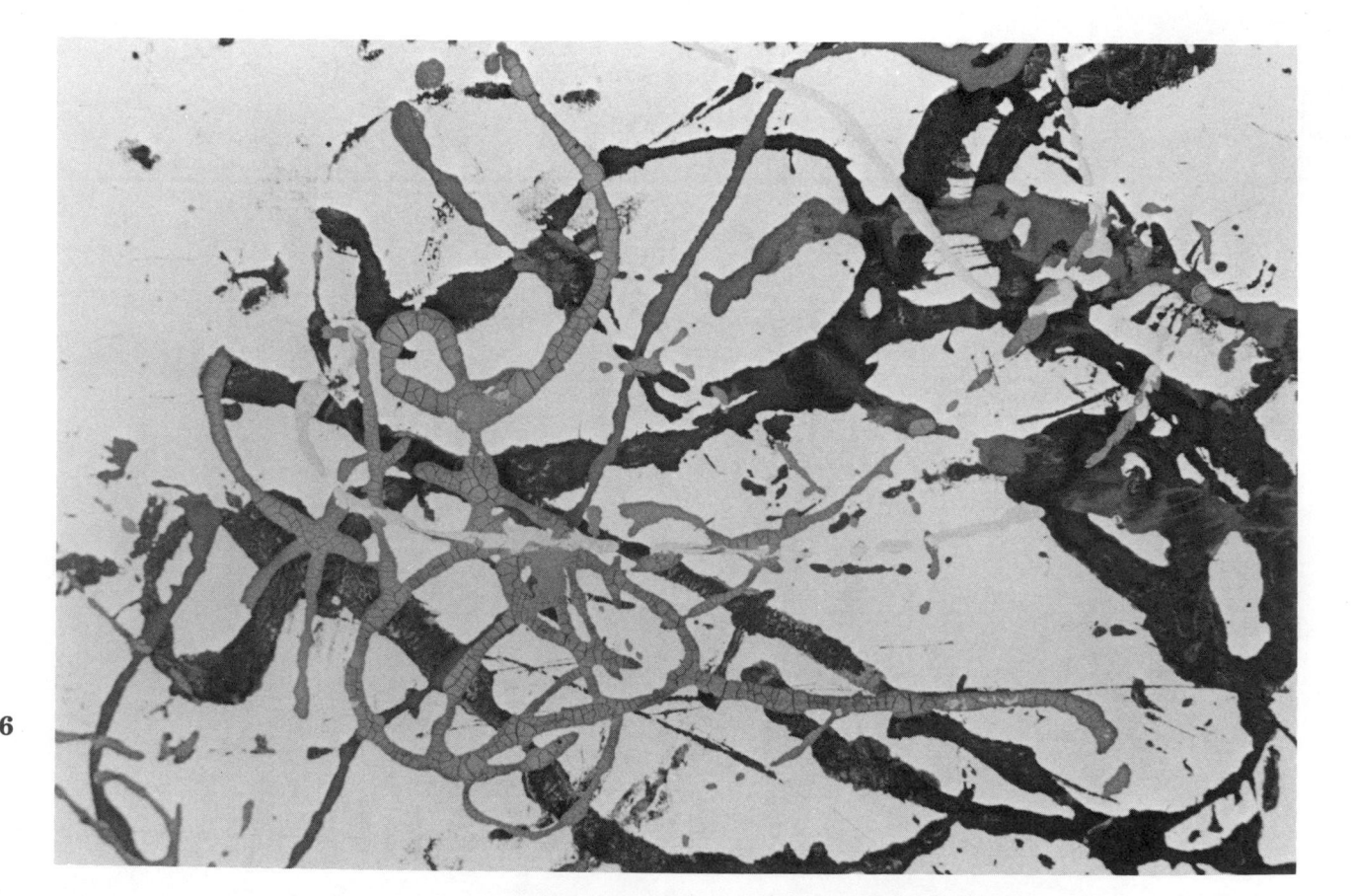

By Elicia, age 6

String Painting

MATERIALS
- White paper
- Tempera paint in bowls
- String

1

Provide one 12" length of string for each bowl of tempera paint.

2

Holding one end, dip string into paint.

3

Lay string onto paper to create design.

4

Redip and relay . . .

5

or use a new string and a new color.

6

VARIATION: Try dropping string onto paper.

7

For a strongly imprinted design, press a second sheet of paper on top of your string design.

Activity 16 • Sand Painting

Age Level: Preschool and up

Notes:

- Sand painting adds the intriguing element of texture to painting with watercolors. Paintings come alive to the eye and to the touch as this new element is introduced.

- Older children may want to pencil-draw a design onto paper first, and decide ahead of time which areas are to be textured by sand. Glue and sand may then be applied to these areas before watercolor is applied.

- Sand may also be used on three-dimensional work to create texture, such as applying it to papier-mâché masks or puppets, before the final coat of paint is applied.

- For another use of sand, see Activity 66, "Sand and Cornstarch Sculpture."

- A sheet of paper placed in the bottom of the tray can be easily lifted out and sand poured back into the original container for recycling.

By Daria, age 4

Sand Painting

MATERIALS
- Dry sand*
- White, medium weight paper
- Paintbrushes
- White glue in small jars
- Large tray or cookie sheet for shaking off sand

OPTIONAL
- Watercolors
- Watercolor brushes
- Container of water
- White glue in small squeeze bottle

*White beach sand preferred.

1

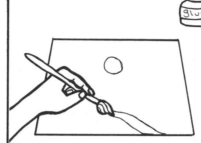

With brush, paint white glue onto paper to make design or picture.

2

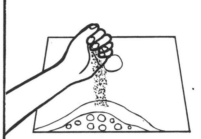

Sprinkle sand onto the paper.

3

Continue sprinkling sand until all glue areas are covered.

4

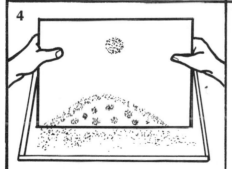

Shake loose sand into tray.

5

Allow to dry.

6

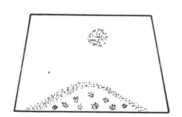

If desired, paint sand picture with watercolors around or on sand.

7

VARIATION: Squirt glue from small squeeze bottle instead of brushing glue on. Proceed as above.

Activity 17 • Snow Painting

Age Level: Preschool and up

Notes:

- This makes a great project on a snowy day or to help channel children's excitement over the first snowstorm of the year.

- Another "snow" related project is Activity 64, "Soapsuds Sculpture."
- Activity 16, "Sand Painting," might be introduced near this time as they involve a similar technique.

By Aaron, age 4

Snow Painting

MATERIALS
- White soap powder, such as Ivory Snow®
- Cookie sheet or tray
- Colored construction paper
- White tempera in jar
- Paint brush

OPTIONAL
- Cotton balls
- White glue
- Colored chalk

1 Pour soap powder onto cookie sheet.

2 Using hands, spread powder out to cover surface of cookie sheet.

3 Paint a design or picture onto colored construction paper using white tempera paint.

4 Place paper, painted-side down, in tray of soap power.

5 Press paper to tray.

6 Remove paper from tray and allow to dry.

7 VARIATIONS: (1) Try gluing cotton balls to snow painting. (2) Try doing a snow painting on black paper. (3) Draw a chalk picture on blank paper before using white tempera and soap powder.

Activity 18 • Encaustic

Age Level: First grade and up

Notes:

- IMPORTANT: Before attempting this project, read "Precautions on Using Hot Wax" in Section One.
- This project can only be attempted with younger children in a *highly supervised,* small-group situation. Very young children should never be left alone with hot fry pan or wax. An adult should help them through the project.
- If children become very interested in melted wax, you might also want to try other projects that use wax. (See Activity 27, "Paper Batik"; Activity 28, "Batik"; and Activity 65, "Wax Sculptures.")

By Bekah, age 4

Encaustic

	1	**2**	**3**
MATERIALS • Old electric fry pan • Pitcher of water • Cupcake tin to fit fry pan • Bits of paraffin wax • Crayons or crayon chips • Cotton swabs • Small size white mat board or heavy white paper **WARNING** • Do *not* attempt this project without first reading "Precautions on Using Hot Wax."	 Place crayon chips in cups, one color in each. Add a small amount of paraffin to dilute color intensity.	 Fill electric fry pan with water. Heat to 225° fahrenheit.	 Rest cupcake tin on sides of fry pan so that cup bottoms touch water surface.

4	**5**	**6**	**7**
 Place cotton swab in each cup. Allow wax to melt.	 Paint melted wax on paper or cardboard using a different cotton swab for each color.	Try filling the whole space with color, or try drawing a specific object on a white background.	Be sure all the water does not boil out of the pan, and change cotton swabs when dirty or worn.

Activity 19 • Egg Tempera

Age Level: Preschool and up

Notes:

- With this project can come a discussion of paint. What is it? Where does it come from? How is it made?
- You can also discuss dyes. How are dyes made? What is the difference between paints and dyes?

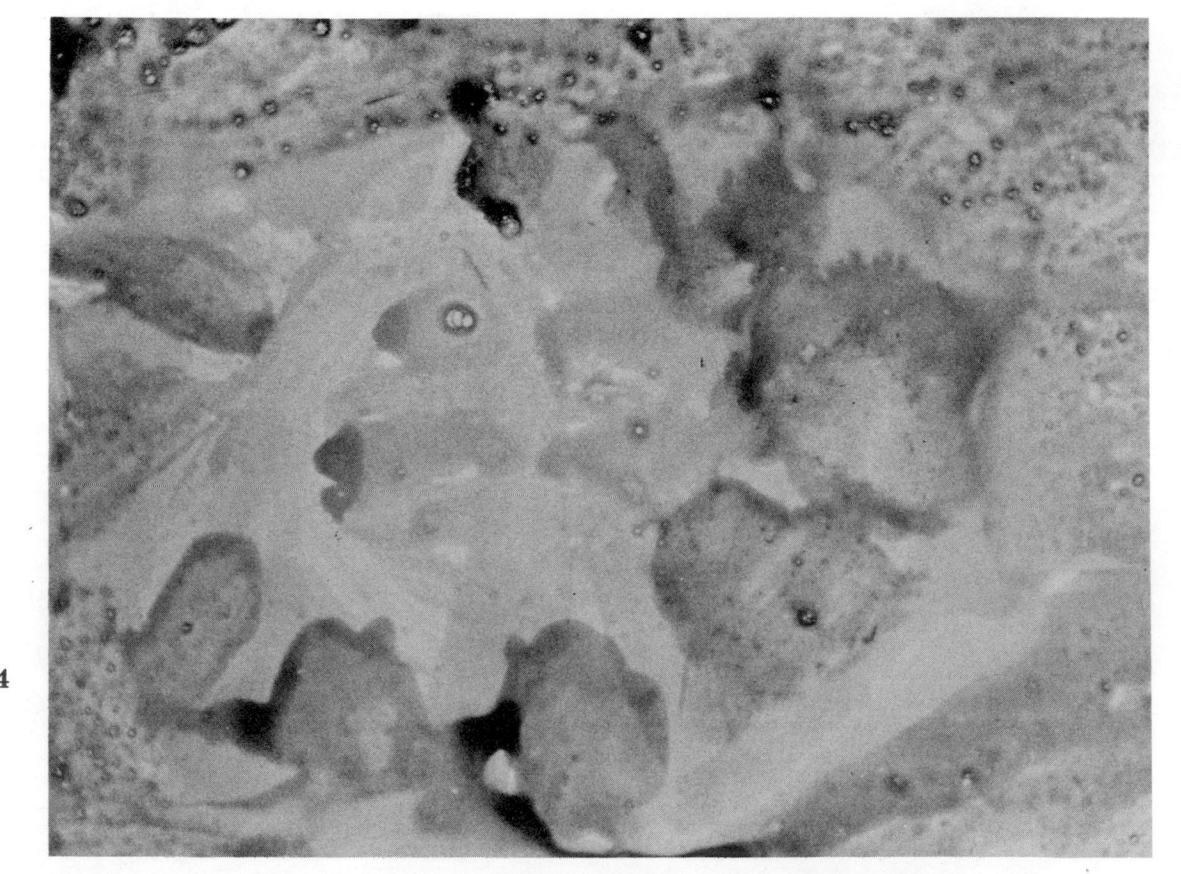

By Aaron, age 4

Egg Tempera

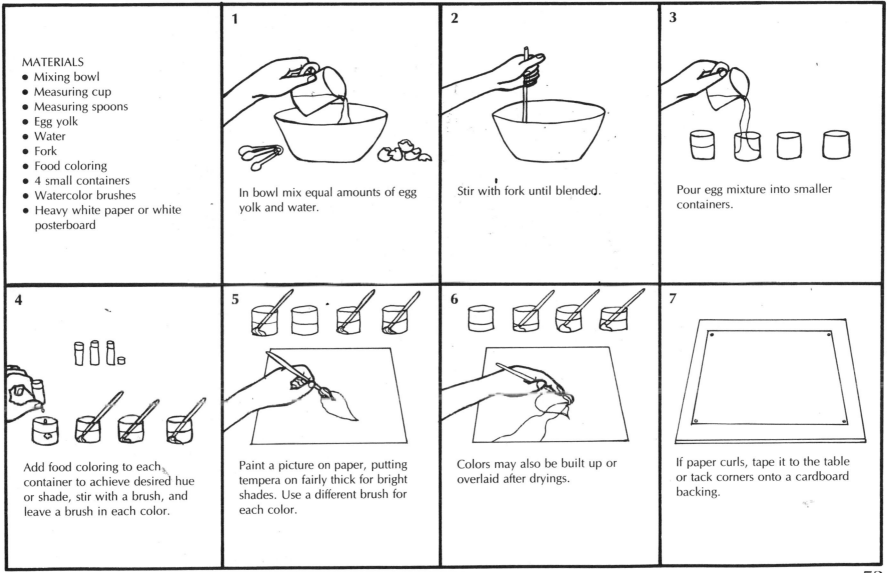

MATERIALS
- Mixing bowl
- Measuring cup
- Measuring spoons
- Egg yolk
- Water
- Fork
- Food coloring
- 4 small containers
- Watercolor brushes
- Heavy white paper or white posterboard

1 In bowl mix equal amounts of egg yolk and water.

2 Stir with fork until blended.

3 Pour egg mixture into smaller containers.

4 Add food coloring to each container to achieve desired hue or shade, stir with a brush, and leave a brush in each color.

5 Paint a picture on paper, putting tempera on fairly thick for bright shades. Use a different brush for each color.

6 Colors may also be built up or overlaid after dryings.

7 If paper curls, tape it to the table or tack corners onto a cardboard backing.

53

Activity 20 • Napkin Dyeing

Age Level: Preschool and up

Notes:

- These pictures are most attractive when the entire napkin surface is covered with food coloring.
- Dyed napkins can be ironed, then glued to a surface with rubber cement glue and matted.

- Children might also try finding their favorite area of their picture and cutting it out to mat as a small picture, or to glue onto a card front.

- Young children sometimes like to tape these dyeings to the window and let the light shine through them.

By Jennifer, age 5

Napkin Dyeing

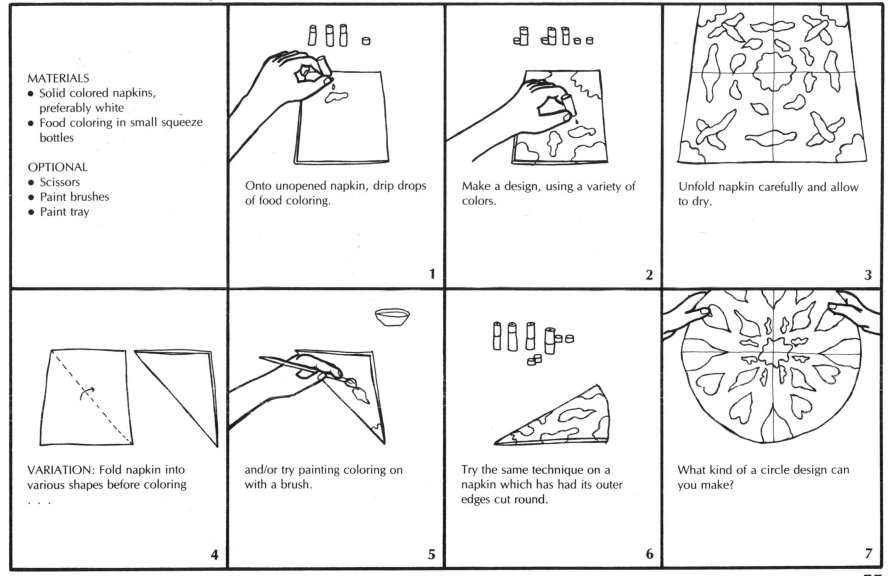

MATERIALS
- Solid colored napkins, preferably white
- Food coloring in small squeeze bottles

OPTIONAL
- Scissors
- Paint brushes
- Paint tray

1 Onto unopened napkin, drip drops of food coloring.

2 Make a design, using a variety of colors.

3 Unfold napkin carefully and allow to dry.

4 VARIATION: Fold napkin into various shapes before coloring . . .

5 and/or try painting coloring on with a brush.

6 Try the same technique on a napkin which has had its outer edges cut round.

7 What kind of a circle design can you make?

55

Activity 21 • Tie Dye T-Shirt
Age Level: Preschool and up

Notes:

- Young children enjoy this project, although they will need varying degrees of help. They can bunch up the cloth themselves, but will need help tightly wrapping string or elastic bands.

- Household dyes, such as Rit® or Tintex®, may be used but they are not colorfast. Cold-water fabric dyes, such as Hi-Dye® or Dylon®, are colorfast. In either case, dye should be mixed according to the package directions. Dye cloth slightly darker than desired color as it lightens as it dries.

- When mixing dyes (which should be done *only* by an adult), a paper mask worn over the nose and mouth will prevent dust particles from being inhaled. These masks are available in hardware stores.

- Rubber gloves should be worn at all times during the dyeing process.

- For the best results, use at least two colors of dye, choosing colors that will blend well when dyed over each other (such as red and blue, yellow and blue, yellow and red, etc.). Generally, dye from light to dark unless you have a specific reason not to, such as wanting to create a blue and green color scheme by dyeing yellow over blue.

- For an added challenge, try batiking on top of a tie-dyed background and then dyeing the shirt a final dark color that will add crackle lines to the dyed shirt.

By Misa, age 6

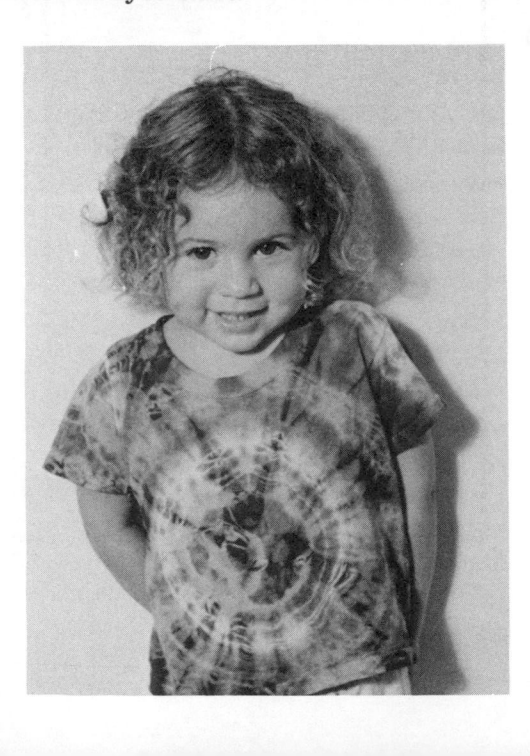

By Shana, age 3

Tie Dye T-shirt

MATERIALS
- Prewashed 100% cotton T-shirt
- Thick rubber bands
- String
- Scissors
- Dye
- Plastic dye basin
- Rubber gloves
- Stick or stirring spoon

1 Separating front and back of shirt, bunch up areas of shirt . . .

2 and wrap them tightly with rubber bands or string.

3 Repeat this in several areas of the shirt.

4 Mix dye bath according to directions. Place shirt in bath until desired color is achieved.

5 Using rubber gloves, squeeze out excess dye. Hang to dry.

6 Repeat bunching and wrapping process on top of newly dyed color. Then dye a second color.

7 After final dyeing, rinse shirt in cold water, squeeze, and hang to dry. Remove string and rubber bands.

Activity 22 • Marbling

Age Level: First grade and up

Notes:

- This is an unusual and exciting process used long ago to make book covers and book liners.
- Marbling is exciting for all ages, children *and* adults, as it creates such exquisite designs so simply.

- Smocks are a must for this project because oil-base inks do not wash off clothing.
- This project guarantees great results, but needs to be closely supervised by an adult.
- A cloth dipped in paint thinner and kept nearby is handy for cleaning up paint on hands.

By Gretchen, age 4

Marbling

MATERIALS
- Large disposable tray with 1½" high sides
- Oil base ink or paint; 2 or 3 colors
- Plastic spoons
- Wooden stirrers
- Rag with paint thinner for cleanup
- White construction paper cut to fit in tray
- Water
- Paper bag for stirrer disposal
- Baby food jars

1. Fill tray with one inch of water. Put ink in jars next to tray.

2. Spoon colors onto surface of water. Return spoons to appropriate jars.

3. When all the colors have been added, gently stir water with wooden stick. If ink sinks to bottom of tray, it needs to be thinned with turpentine.

4. Hold paper flat above tray. Watch swirling design form.

5. When you see a design you like, drop paper onto surface of water.

6. Watch paper absorb ink. Be sure edges and corners touch water.

7. Swiftly remove paper from tray, picking up by one corner. Lay flat to dry.

Activity 23 • Fresco

Age Level: Preschool and up

Notes:

- Plaster of paris is a unique and intriguing material. A brave adult may want to set up a time when children can just "play" with plaster without a specific goal in mind, just to acquaint children with its unusual properties.

- Frescoes can be done in conjunction with other plaster of paris projects. (See Activity 7, "Plaster Scratchboard.")

- Plaster of paris dries quickly so get well organized before the plaster is mixed. There is little time to spare!

By Matthew, age 4

Fresco

MATERIALS
- Large mixing bowl
- Measuring cups
- Plaster of paris
- Pitcher of water
- Large wooden spoon
- Styrofoam® or cardboard food trays with 1" sides
- Watercolors
- Watercolor brushes
- Jar of water
- Paper towels

1
In large mixing bowl, mix plaster and water according to package directions.

2
Quickly stir to dissolve plaster using large wooden spoon.

3
Pour plaster immediately into food tray(s).

4
If plaster is thick, shake tray(s) to level surface.

5
METHOD 1: Before plaster hardens, paint on and in plaster mixture using brush strokes to create texture in plaster. Allow to set.

6
METHOD 2: When plaster has set, paint picture or design on the plaster surface.

7
NOTE: Plaster of paris offers a wide variety of routes for creative exploration, but it is messy to work with and takes time and patience to learn how best to use it. Give it a try when you are in the mood. Your kids will find it totally seductive.

61

RESIST

Resist is the application of two non-combining materials to a common surface. When applied on top of or beside each other, these materials do not mix or blend, but rather "resist" each other.

The resist process is delightful. The materials themselves are irresistable: gooey glue, slippery wax, runny melted crayon. These materials may initially be the most compelling aspect of the resist experience for the young child. So, despite the fact that the child has already been primed for resist through painting experiences, don't be surprised to find at first an entire piece of paper smeared with white glue, or a piece of cloth stiffened into a solid sheet of wax. These early explorations are important to the child's artistic process. When a child engrossed in resist is asked, "What happens to the paint when it touches the glue?", he or she may answer with, "It sparkles!" This is a valid response. Only later will the child come to understand why it sparkles (the glue resists the paint). Later still, the child can be encouraged toward a more delicate use of these materials.

IMPORTANT; Before starting any resist activity, refer to the precautions listed in Section One regarding hot wax.

Notes on Batik

Batik is a more complex resist process that is introduced in Activity 40. It requires the alternate application of hot wax and dye to cotton cloth. This process creates images that are actually dyed into the fabric. Traditionally, batik fabrics have been made for centuries in the East using a very elaborate and time-consuming process. With modern tools and technology, batik can be accomplished quite simply and quickly, and is fun for people of all ages. Young children become very excited about batik, both for its novelty and the responsibility they are given in doing this work. When working with young children however, strict adult supervision is a must. They should not have free access to the frypan or the wax, and they should be closely assisted at all steps.

Before attempting projects in batik, review the following information.

Wax. Batik may be done with paraffin wax, or with a combination of paraffin and beeswax. Beeswax smells very sweet, is expensive, and is a softer, more pliable wax. A softer wax will create less of a crackle effect on the batik, as the wax will not crack as easily when the cloth is crumpled. Selection of wax is a matter of aesthetic preference, availability, and cost. Beeswax is often sold at art supply stores or can be obtained from a local beekeeper. Paraffin wax is sold at most grocery stores.

Tools. Hot wax may be applied to the cloth with either a tjanting tool or a paint brush. Application procedures and results differ for each instrument.

Tjanting. A tjanting tool is used to make wax lines. The word "tjanting" is an Indonesian word meaning "writing in wax." To use a tjanting, first let its metal bowl warm briefly in the melted wax. Next, grip the wooden handle and scoop the

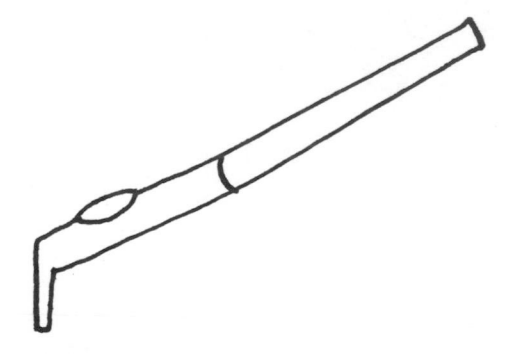

hot wax into the bowl of the tjanting. Wax will dribble out of the hollow tube to create wax lines. Guide the tjanting over the cloth to create the desired design.

The tjanting makes either lines or dots depending on the temperature and flow of the wax. Cooler wax flows more slowly and tends to make dots. Warmer wax flows faster and creates solid lines. A tjanting must be returned frequently to the hot wax as the narrow tubing cools rapidly and inhibits wax flow.

A tjanting can be purchased at an art supply store, and is relatively inexpensive.

Paint brush. An inexpensive paint brush, either of the artist's or house painter's variety, is appropriate when working with children. A fairly thick watercolor brush works well or a half-inch painter's brush. Make sure that the brush handle is wooden as a plastic handle can be melted by the heat of the frypan.

The tjanting is more difficult to use. For this reason, the paint brush is preferred for young children, though sometimes even the youngest children may enjoy trying the exotic tjanting tool, with adult help.

Preventing tool slippage. To prevent waxing tools from slipping into the pan of hot wax, take an empty tuna fish can, cut off both top and bottom, wash, and place the remaining metal ring in the frypan with the melted wax. Replace the waxing tool(s) inside the metal ring after each use.

Dyes. "Procion" is a generic term for good quality, cold water dyes that will not wash out or fade. Two highly recommended procion dye brands are Hi-Dye® and Dylon®. Rit® and Tintex® are hot water dyes that are neither color-fast nor light-proof. These dyes may be used with cold water for batik projects. If they are used with hot water as directed on the package the water will melt the wax from the cloth. Hi-Dye® and Dylon® dyes can be purchased at a local art supply store or arts and crafts shop. Rit® and Tintex® are available at supermarkets and general merchandise stores.

Choosing dye colors. A batik color scheme is created by the alternate layering of wax and dyes. Because the cloth is submerged in sequential dye baths, it is important that the chosen dye colors blend well together. Some suggested color combinations are: yellow, orange, and red (or brown); yellow, green, and blue; and red and blue in that order. Whatever colors are chosen, remember that each dying is affected by the underlying cloth color. Blue dyed over red will create purple, for instance, while blue dyed over yellow will create green. As a rule, encourage children to order their dye baths from light to dark, unless they have a specific reason to do otherwise. This will create the greatest color contrast and will accentuate the crackle effect.

Work area. When batiking with young children, it is wise to set up the project in a remote corner of the room and line the walls, tabletop, and floors with newspaper. Protecting the waxing, dying, and drying areas will make the job of cleaning up a lot easier. Here is a suggested set-up for the waxing area:

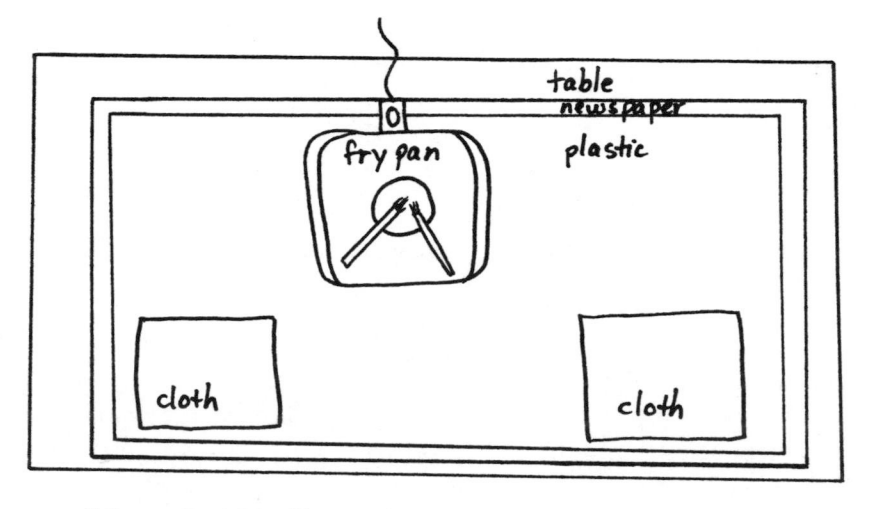

Ideas for batik projects. Batik creations are varied and lovely. Wallhangings, matted pictures, greeting cards, pillows, patchwork wallhangings and T- shirts are some of the things that young children can make.

NOTES ON ANDREA: FINDING HER WAY

Andrea, age 8, is having difficulty applying herself to the class project: book illustrations with crayon resist. Although I feel that her initial drawings and paintings are successful, she insists that they are "no good" and refuses to work on her book. My gentle encouragement only seems to upset her further. She cries, telling me once again that her pictures are "no good." At a loss to help ease her own critical self-judgment, I leave her alone. She fritters away class time by daydreaming. Finally, she begins to doodle. Beginning with the letter A in the center of her paper, she continues to draw A's, connecting one to another all over her paper. She weaves a most intricate spider web. This work seems almost effortless in contrast to her earlier struggles. It is as if her spider web is an extension of her daydream.

Later in the year, I begin a batik unit by having the children first sketch a picture on paper and then on cloth before applying the wax. Lifelessly, Andrea fulfills the assignment, barely able to complete it. She appears disinterested and, while the other children choose to do several batiks, she returns to daydreaming. She wastes more time, until the day I announce the final waxing session. On her own initiative, she approaches the waxing area. She takes a piece of cloth and begins to doodle with wax. She waxes a heart in the center of her cloth, then effortlessly extends lines out to a pattern to create an intricate abstract design similar in style to her spider web. Her enthusiasm sparked, she begins to play more freely. She drips and splatters wax across a new piece of cloth, creating a batik design full of life and energy. Pleased, she makes more and more batiks, each one a new experiment in "splatter batik." Each is rich in movement and design. Andrea has found her way.

Activity 24 • Crayon Resist

Age Level: Preschool and up

Notes:

- This is the most simple form of resist and just the beginning of a truly eye-opening experience for children. Let children try this project several times, as the beginning of a whole series of resist projects. Watch the spark of discovery and understanding take hold as children explore the resist process through many different materials.

- Be sure to tell the children to press their crayons firmly against the paper as they draw to insure creation of the resist effect.

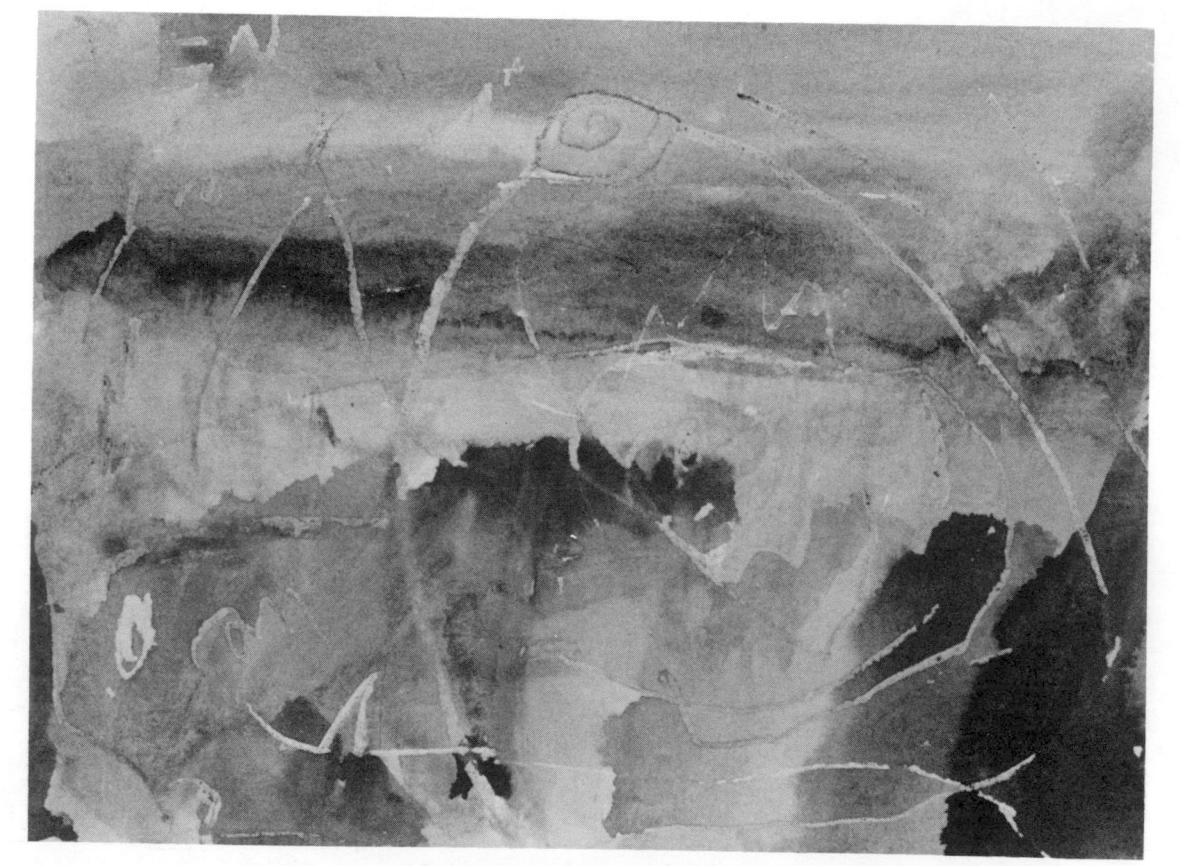

By Jennifer, age 4

Crayon Resist

MATERIALS
- White construction paper
- Crayons
- Watercolors
- Watercolor brushes
- Glass of water
- Paper towels

OPTIONAL
- Black ink
- Sponge brush
- Small bowl

1 Pressing down firmly with crayon, draw a design or picture on a piece of paper.

2 Paint with watercolors on and around crayon design.

3 Try to paint entire page.

4 VARIATION: Pressing down firmly with crayons, draw a picture or design on a piece of paper.

5 Brush black ink across the entire paper with a sponge brush. Allow to dry.

6 Try making pictures, coloring in large solid areas with crayon and then inking paper. . .

7 or making line drawings with crayon and then painting picture.

Activity 25 • Cray-Pas® Resist

Age Level: Preschool and up

Notes:

- Cray-Pas® resist presents a slight variation from crayon resist. Can the students figure out how they are alike? How they are different?

- Cray-Pas® can also be used in combination with watercolors as in Activity 24, "Crayon Resist."

- Have children experiment with combining both crayon resist and Cray-Pas® resist in one work of art. What effect does this create?

By Meredith, age 6

Cray-pas® Resist

MATERIALS
- Heavy white paper
- Cray-Pas®
- Thinned black tempera in bowl
- Sponge brush or paint brush
- Paper towels

OPTIONAL
- White tempera
- Colored tempera
- Black ink
- Crayons

1

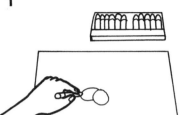

With Cray-Pas®, make a design which covers the entire paper.

2

Brush layers of thinned black tempera over picture.

3

While paint is still wet, excess paint may be dabbed with paper towel.

4

Paper towel dabbing can itself create interesting textures on picture.

5

VARIATION 1: Try using white or colored tempera instead of black.

6

VARIATION 2: Try covering Cray-Pas® design with black ink wash instead of tempera.

7

VARIATION 3: Try using both Cray-Pas® and crayons in initial picture before coating it with black tempera or ink.

Activity 26 • White Glue Resist

Age Level: Preschool and up

Notes:

- When children "draw" with white glue, it becomes transparent as it dries. Because a child's drawing "disappears" with transparency, it is a delightful surprise for them to watch their drawings reappear as they paint over the glue.
- This is a favorite project. Allow children to experience this activity more than once.

- This project can be combined with other activities. (See Activity 16, "Sand Painting," and Activity 24, "Crayon Resist.")
- This project requires two working periods with time in between for the glue to dry thoroughly.

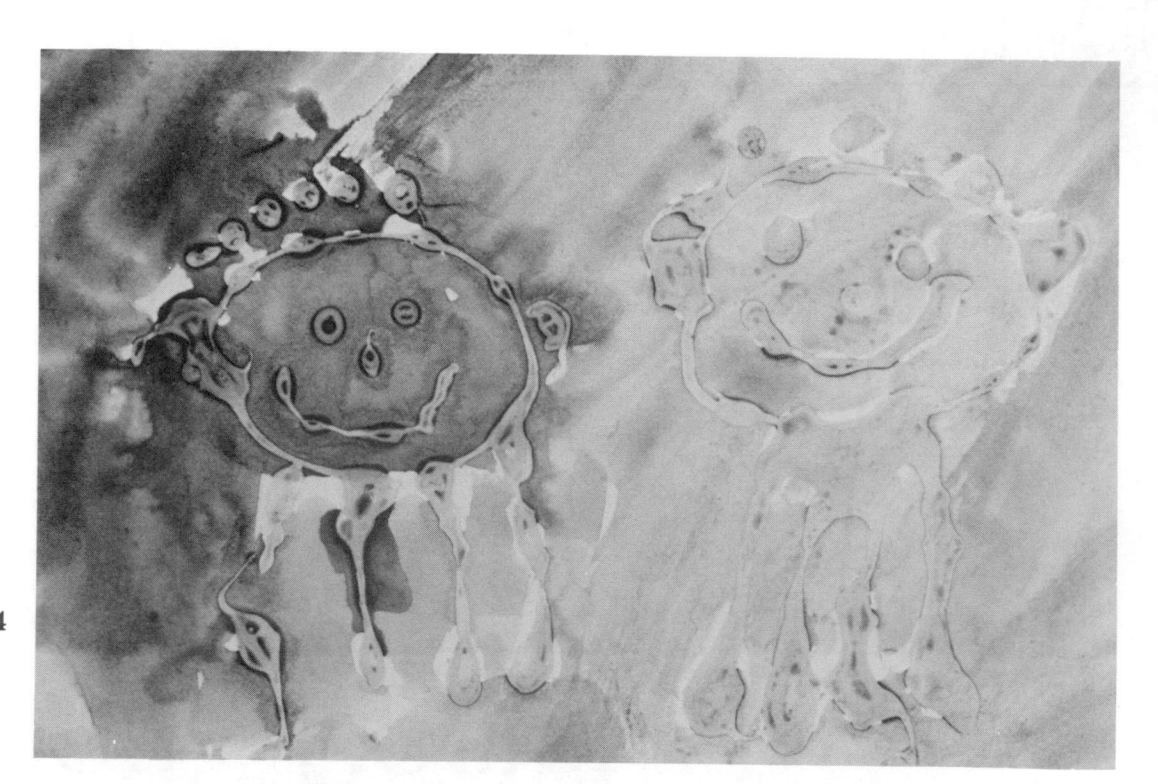

By Kate, age 4

White Glue Resist

MATERIALS
- Small squeeze bottle of white glue
- White construction paper
- Premoistened watercolors
- Watercolor brushes
- Glass of water

OPTIONAL
- Glue in baby food jar
- Watercolor brush for glue
- Sand, salt, sawdust, sugar, etc.

1

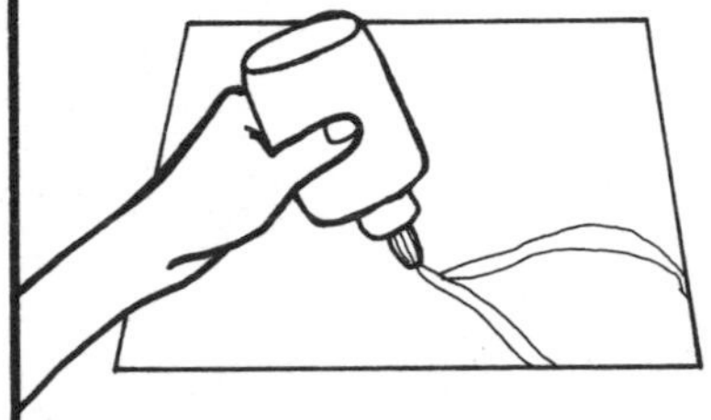

Hold glue bottle upside down. Squeeze and draw design or picture with glue.

2

Lay flat to dry.

3

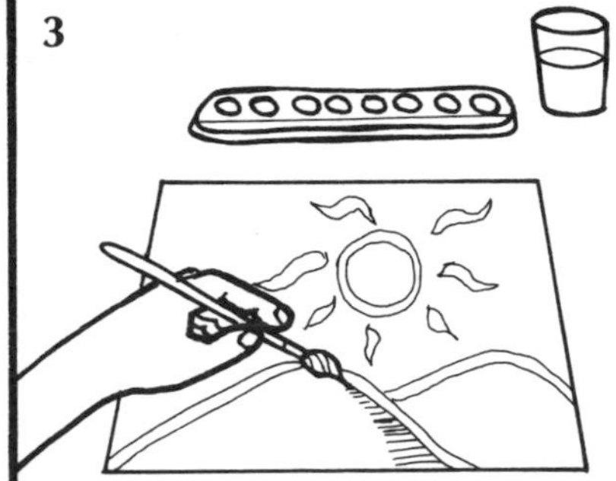

With watercolors, paint on and around glue.

4

Try painting the entire paper to highlight the glue design.

5

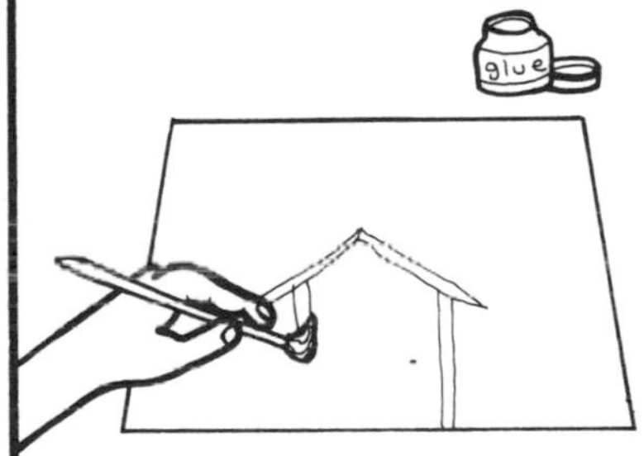

VARIATION: Paint glue on with a brush. . .

6

sprinkle sand, sugar, salt, sawdust, etc., onto wet glue.

7

Shake off excess. Allow to dry and then paint.

Activity 27 • Paper Batik

Age Level: First grade and up

Notes:

- IMPORTANT: Before attempting this project, read the precautions in Section One.

- When glued to a heavier folded paper, these pictures make lovely cards and gifts.

- Although this is not the real batik process, it introduces children to working with wax and creates an interesting effect in its own right.

- CAUTION: This project may be attempted by younger children *only* in well-supervised, small-group situations. Younger children should *not* have free access to frypan or hot wax.

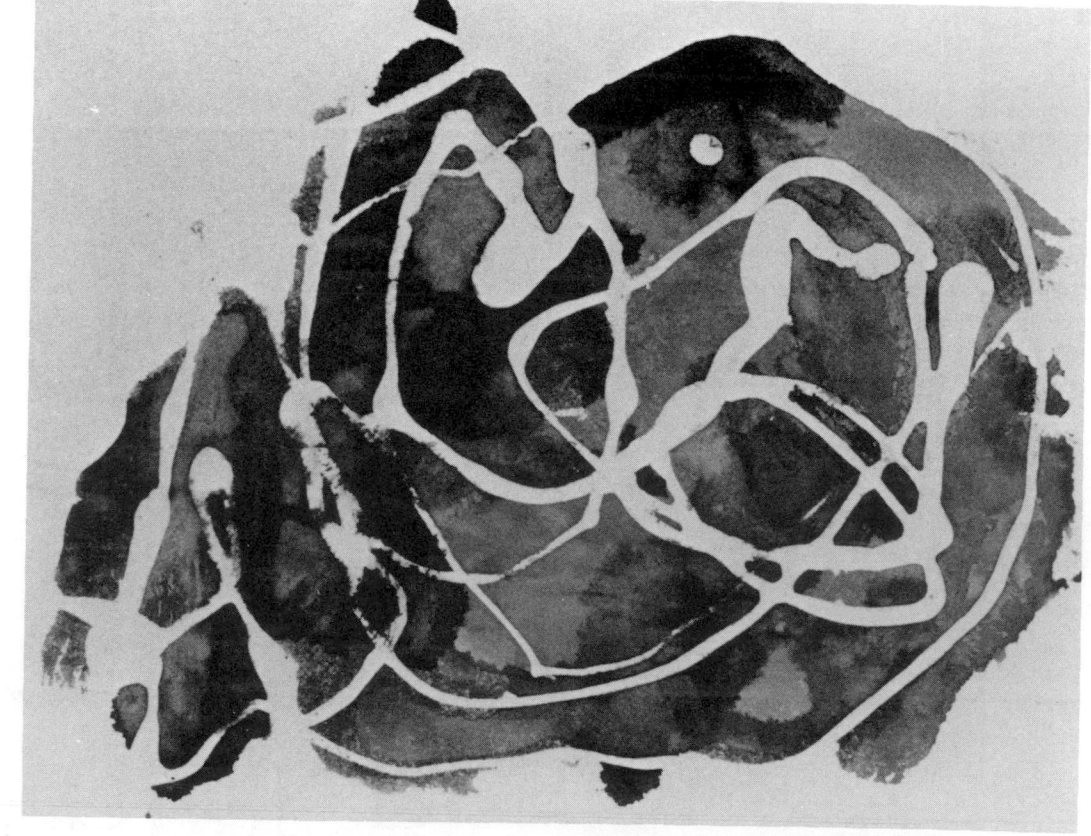

By Matthew, age 4

Paper Batik

MATERIALS
- Unwanted electric fry pan
- Inexpensive rice paper
- Paraffin wax
- Brushes for waxing
- Tjanting tool* (See box 7)
- Watercolors or diluted food coloring
- Watercolor brushes
- Water
- Manila paper or blank newsprint paper
- Iron
- Empty tuna fish can

WARNING: Do not attempt this project without first reading "Precautions in Using Hot Wax." Iron to be used *only* by an adult.

1

Heat enough wax in pan (at 225° F.) to make melted wax at least 1/2 inch deep. Place brushes or tjanting in pan to warm. (An empty tuna fish can can be used to stablize tools.)

2

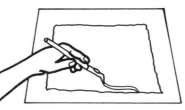

Place rice paper over manila paper or blank newsprint. With melted wax, draw or paint a design on rice paper.

3

Then paint watercolor or diluted food coloring over entire paper.

4

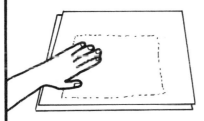

Lay a clean sheet of paper on top of rice paper to make a sandwich effect.

5

With iron on low setting, iron "sandwich" until wax has melted onto outer paper.

6

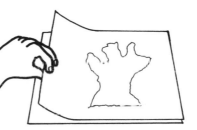

Peel outside papers off picture.

7

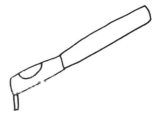

*A tjanting tool can be purchased at a local art supply store. It is used for making wax lines and dots. The tjanting is dipped into the melted wax, scooping wax into its metal bowl. As liquid wax runs out of metal tubing, lines and dots may be draw with it. See box 2 above.

Activity 28 • Batik

Age Level: First grade and up

Notes:

- IMPORTANT: Before attempting this project, read the precautions in Section One, and the notes on batik at the beginning of this section on resist.

- CAUTION: This project may be attempted by younger children *only* in well-supervised, small-group situations. Younger children should *not* have free access to frypan or hot wax.

- When mixing dyes (which should be done by the supervising adult), wear a paper mask over the mouth and nose to prevent the inhalation of dye particles. Rubber gloves must also be worn.

By Misa, age 6

Batik: Waxing

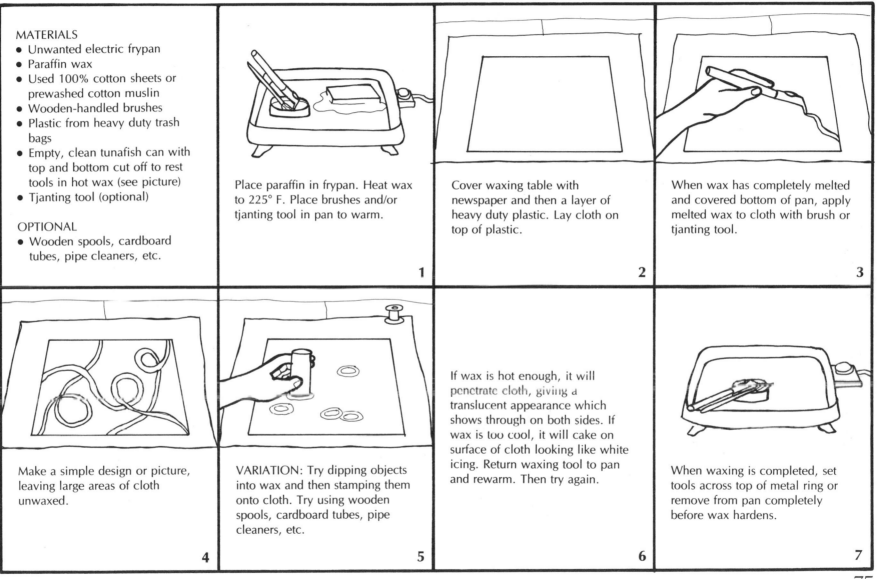

MATERIALS
- Unwanted electric frypan
- Paraffin wax
- Used 100% cotton sheets or prewashed cotton muslin
- Wooden-handled brushes
- Plastic from heavy duty trash bags
- Empty, clean tunafish can with top and bottom cut off to rest tools in hot wax (see picture)
- Tjanting tool (optional)

OPTIONAL
- Wooden spools, cardboard tubes, pipe cleaners, etc.

1 Place paraffin in frypan. Heat wax to 225° F. Place brushes and/or tjanting tool in pan to warm.

2 Cover waxing table with newspaper and then a layer of heavy duty plastic. Lay cloth on top of plastic.

3 When wax has completely melted and covered bottom of pan, apply melted wax to cloth with brush or tjanting tool.

4 Make a simple design or picture, leaving large areas of cloth unwaxed.

5 VARIATION: Try dipping objects into wax and then stamping them onto cloth. Try using wooden spools, cardboard tubes, pipe cleaners, etc.

6 If wax is hot enough, it will penetrate cloth, giving a translucent appearance which shows through on both sides. If wax is too cool, it will cake on surface of cloth looking like white icing. Return waxing tool to pan and rewarm. Then try again.

7 When waxing is completed, set tools across top of metal ring or remove from pan completely before wax hardens.

Batik: Dyeing

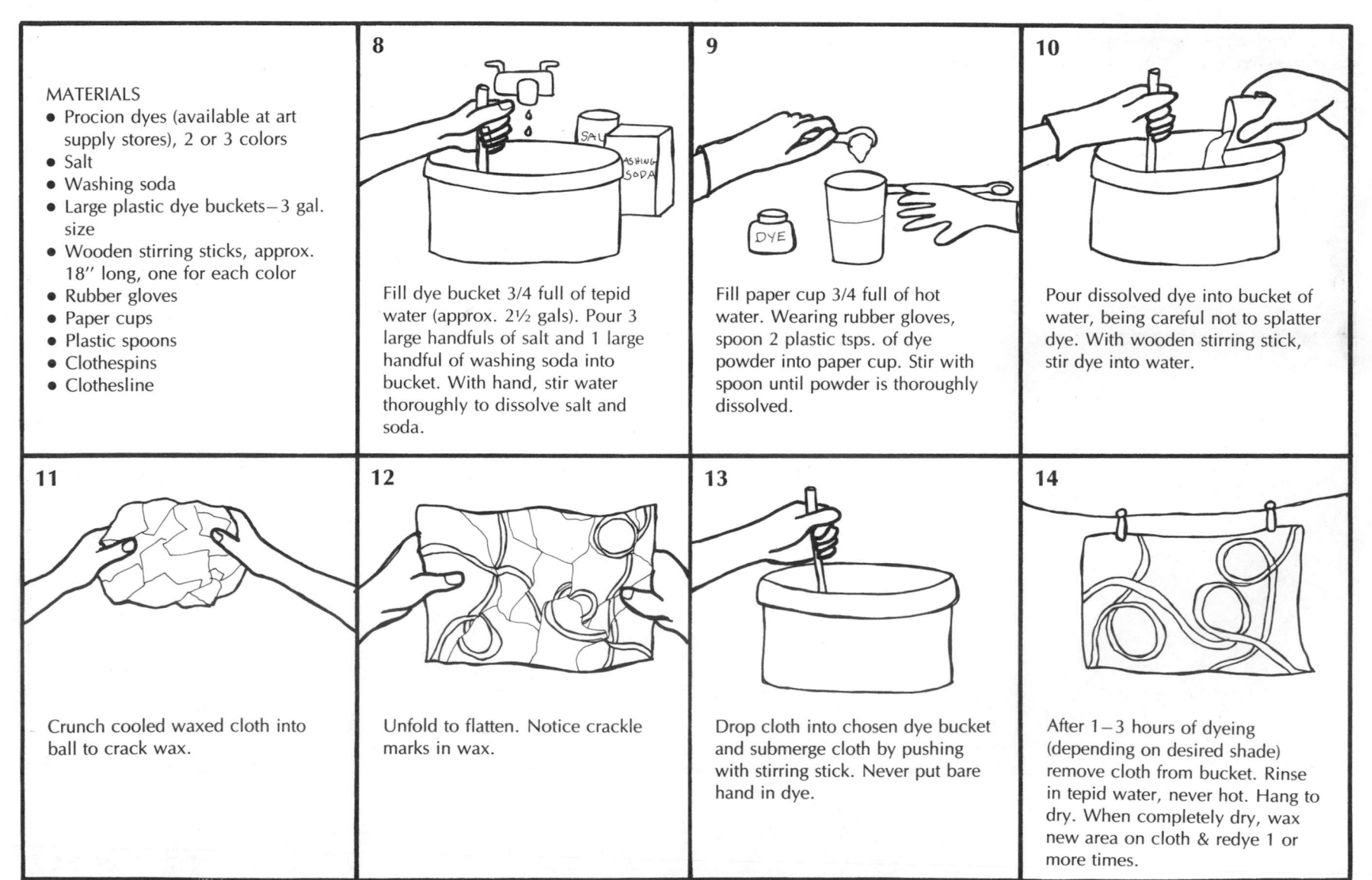

MATERIALS
- Procion dyes (available at art supply stores), 2 or 3 colors
- Salt
- Washing soda
- Large plastic dye buckets—3 gal. size
- Wooden stirring sticks, approx. 18" long, one for each color
- Rubber gloves
- Paper cups
- Plastic spoons
- Clothespins
- Clothesline

8 Fill dye bucket 3/4 full of tepid water (approx. 2½ gals). Pour 3 large handfuls of salt and 1 large handful of washing soda into bucket. With hand, stir water thoroughly to dissolve salt and soda.

9 Fill paper cup 3/4 full of hot water. Wearing rubber gloves, spoon 2 plastic tsps. of dye powder into paper cup. Stir with spoon until powder is thoroughly dissolved.

10 Pour dissolved dye into bucket of water, being careful not to splatter dye. With wooden stirring stick, stir dye into water.

11 Crunch cooled waxed cloth into ball to crack wax.

12 Unfold to flatten. Notice crackle marks in wax.

13 Drop cloth into chosen dye bucket and submerge cloth by pushing with stirring stick. Never put bare hand in dye.

14 After 1—3 hours of dyeing (depending on desired shade) remove cloth from bucket. Rinse in tepid water, never hot. Hang to dry. When completely dry, wax new area on cloth & redye 1 or more times.

Batik: Wax Removal

MATERIALS

Method 1
- Blank newsprint
- Iron (to be used only by an adult)

Method 2
- Stove
- Large old pot
- Salt
- Water
- Stick
- Clothespins & line

Method 3
- Dry cleaning

15

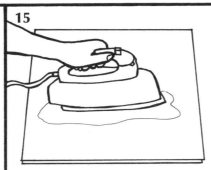

METHOD 1: Sandwich batik between several layers of blank newsprint and iron at a low setting. (Iron to be used by adult only.)

16

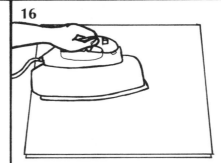

Change papers often until no more wax melts onto them.

17

METHOD 2: In a large pot (not used for cooking) boil water, add a handful of salt. (Young children should not have free access to stove or boiling water.)

18

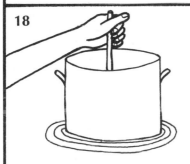

Drop batik into boiling water and stir with stick for no longer than three minutes.

19

Remove batik with stick.

20

Pour water outside, never down the drain. Repeat the process until all the wax is removed. Hang to dry.

21

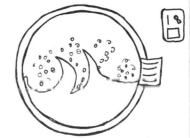

METHOD 3: Put batik into dry cleaning machine or take to a cleaner. Cleaning fluid dissolves wax. This method is the easiest & most efficient.

Activity 29 • Batik Cards

Age Level: First grade and up

Notes:

- IMPORTANT: Before attempting this project, read the precautions in Section One.
- CAUTION: This project should be attempted by younger children *only* in well-supervised, small-group situations. Younger children should *not* be allowed free access to frypan or hot wax.
- IMPORTANT: Rubber cement is toxic and should be used only in a well-ventilated, well-supervised area. In many states, rubber cement is not allowed in elementary classrooms, so check this out first.

By Katy, age 8

Batik Card

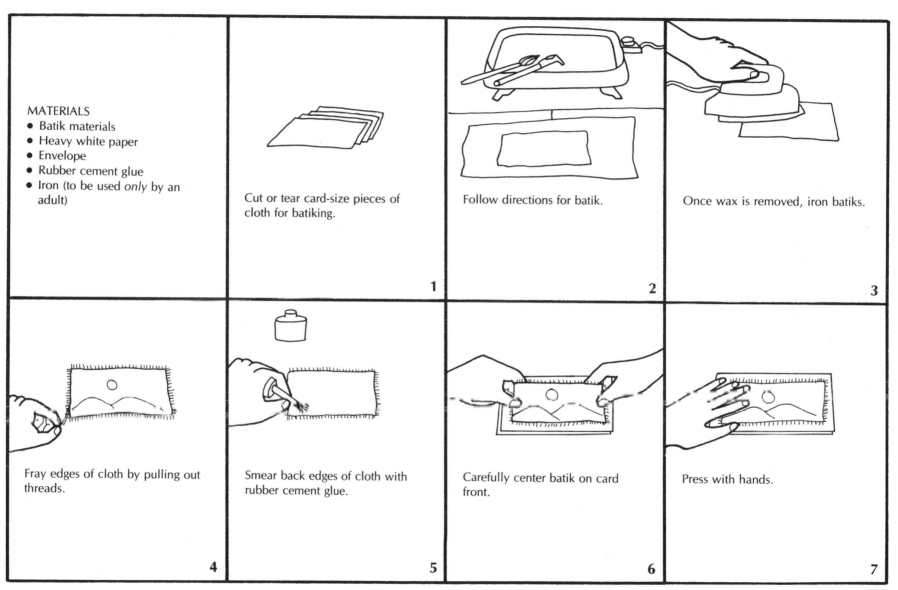

MATERIALS
- Batik materials
- Heavy white paper
- Envelope
- Rubber cement glue
- Iron (to be used *only* by an adult)

Cut or tear card-size pieces of cloth for batiking.

1

Follow directions for batik.

2

Once wax is removed, iron batiks.

3

Fray edges of cloth by pulling out threads.

4

Smear back edges of cloth with rubber cement glue.

5

Carefully center batik on card front.

6

Press with hands.

7

Activity 30 • Batik T-shirt

Age Level: First grade and up

Notes:

- IMPORTANT: Before attempting this project, read the precautions in Section One.

- Cardboard, covered with plastic, is used to keep the wax from the front of the shirt from seeping onto the back of the shirt and vice versa. Cardboard should be cut slightly larger than chest size of the shirt so that the shirt fits snuggly over it.

- These T-shirts make delightful projects and/or gifts. If colorfast dyes are used, designs and colors should last through years of laundering.

- Older children may want to sketch a design on paper beforehand and then pencil draw the design onto the shirt before waxing. Younger children can make lovely spontaneous designs.

- If a design is to be planned, the plan should also include a color scheme so that the same color is not used in adjacent areas.

- CAUTION: Younger children may attempt this project *only* in well-supervised, small-group situations. Children should *not* be allowed free access to frypan or hot wax.

By Misa, age 6

By Shana, age 3

Batik T-shirt

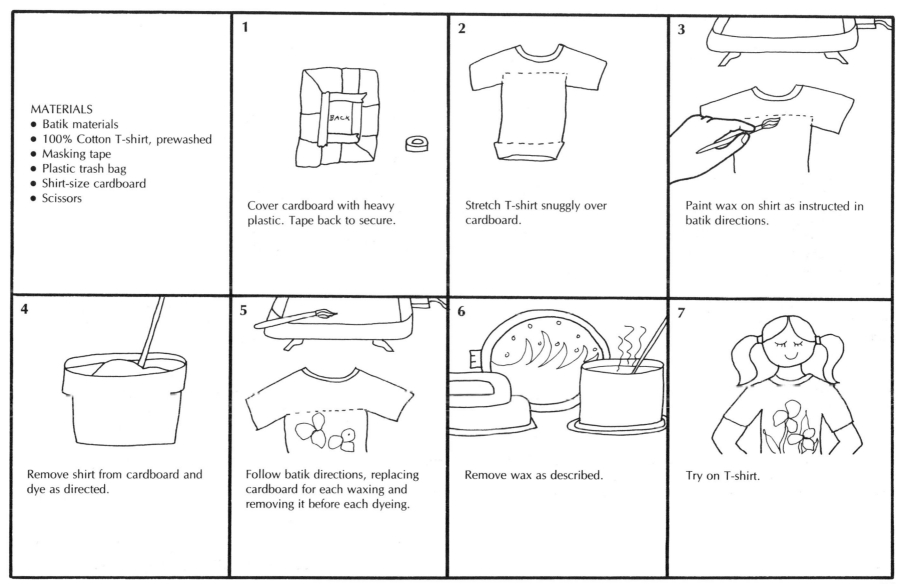

MATERIALS
- Batik materials
- 100% Cotton T-shirt, prewashed
- Masking tape
- Plastic trash bag
- Shirt-size cardboard
- Scissors

1 Cover cardboard with heavy plastic. Tape back to secure.

2 Stretch T-shirt snuggly over cardboard.

3 Paint wax on shirt as instructed in batik directions.

4 Remove shirt from cardboard and dye as directed.

5 Follow batik directions, replacing cardboard for each waxing and removing it before each dyeing.

6 Remove wax as described.

7 Try on T-shirt.

Activity 31 • Batik Puppet

Age Level: Second grade and up

Notes:

- IMPORTANT: Before attempting this project, read the precautions in Section One. Remember cautions about younger children and hot wax/batik projects.
- The basic puppet shape can be varied greatly to offer the possibility of shaping animal ears, hats, etc.
- Puppet backs may be solid colors, solid colors with crackle lines, actual backsides of puppet character, or an entirely different puppet (thus making a "two-character puppet").
- This puppet can be made by younger children if an adult does the sewing.

By Katy, age 8

Batik Puppet

MATERIALS
- Batik materials
- Pencil
- Iron (to be used *only* by an adult)
- Common pins
- Scissors
- Needle
- Thread

OPTIONAL
- Sewing machine

1

Place two 8" squares of prewashed cotton together.

2

Place hand over squares, thumb and little finger spread. Trace around them for puppet shape allowing a 2" margin.

3

Pin inside pencil line. Then cut along line with scissors.

4

Separate cloth pieces. Wax puppet design on them separately, following directions for batik.

5

Once wax is removed, iron pieces. Next pin right sides of batik together. Hand or machine sew around puppet edge, leaving bottom open.

6

Remove pins. With right sides still together, separate and fold up bottom edge and hem.

7

Turn right side out. Try on your puppet!

PRINTING

Printing techniques offer the child two new options: (1) to create an image through the use of found objects, and/or to make homemade stamps, stencils, or prepared "plates," and (2) to reproduce an image repeatedly. For the very young artist who lacks the fine motor skills to either reproduce likenesses or depict decipherable shapes and images, these printing techniques offer a particular thrill. Not only can the child now reproduce imagery, but he or she can also work "representationally."

The printing techniques introduced in this section fall into three categories: stamping, stenciling, and printmaking. Stamping involves the application of paint to one surface of a found object or prepared stamp. This surface is then pressed onto the page. Stenciling requires the application of paint directly to the paper, but within the outline of a stencil form. Printmaking involves the creation of one's own printing surface through the use of simple painting techniques, or through making a printing plate. With each of these techniques, the young artist is challenged to play with aesthetics in a new and fascinating way.

David's Polka Dot Handprints:
A Tale of the Creative Process

I set out halved mushrooms, black and white paper, and two plates—one holding a sponge soaked with white paint, the other holding a sponge soaked with black paint. I ask David if he would like to join me in making a mushroom print. He obliges and sits down to work.

David stamps with the mushrooms, first impressing a black image on white paper and then impressing a white image on black paper. His prints are well executed, but do not seem to excite him.

He pauses for a moment, then grins mischievously. Spreading his fingers over the black sponge, he looks up at me to see if I will stop him. I don't. Delighted, David presses his hand into the black sponge, then slaps it onto his paper. The print pleases him, so he makes another and another. David prints hands up and down, sideways, upside down, and beside each other across the paper. Each new print marks a new experiment and wears a new design.

David eyes the white sponge. He slaps one hand down onto it, then smacks his hand onto the paper. Next, he simultaneously prints one hand of each color—black and white—on the page. Next he presses both hands at once into the paint-soaked sponges and then gleefully rubs his hands together. Smack! A steel-grey print on the page!

There is some pink and blue paint sitting on a nearby table. Excited by David's experimentation, I ask him if he'd like to try using some other colors. He beams and jumps up to get the paints. Quickly, he dabs his steel-grey hands with pink and blue polka dots. Then, Splat! Splat! Splat! More and more prints emerge, each print wilder than the last. There is a creative frenzy, then a sigh. David is done.

Satisfied, he gets up to wash his hands. All that remains is a tabletop covered with prints, each print representing an important step in David's creative journey.

Activity 32 • Handprints

Age Level: Preschool and up

Notes:

- Handprints and footprints are a most basic and relevant form of printing for young children. Try inventing small or large group-projects involving hand and footprints.
- Older children can use their imagination to create intricate designs using hand and footprints.
- This project could be tied into a unit called "About Me" as a record of hand-size. Handprints could be included in "Me" books that could also include self-portraits, drawings of family members, height/weight records, lists of favorite things, photos, stories, and transcribed interviews.

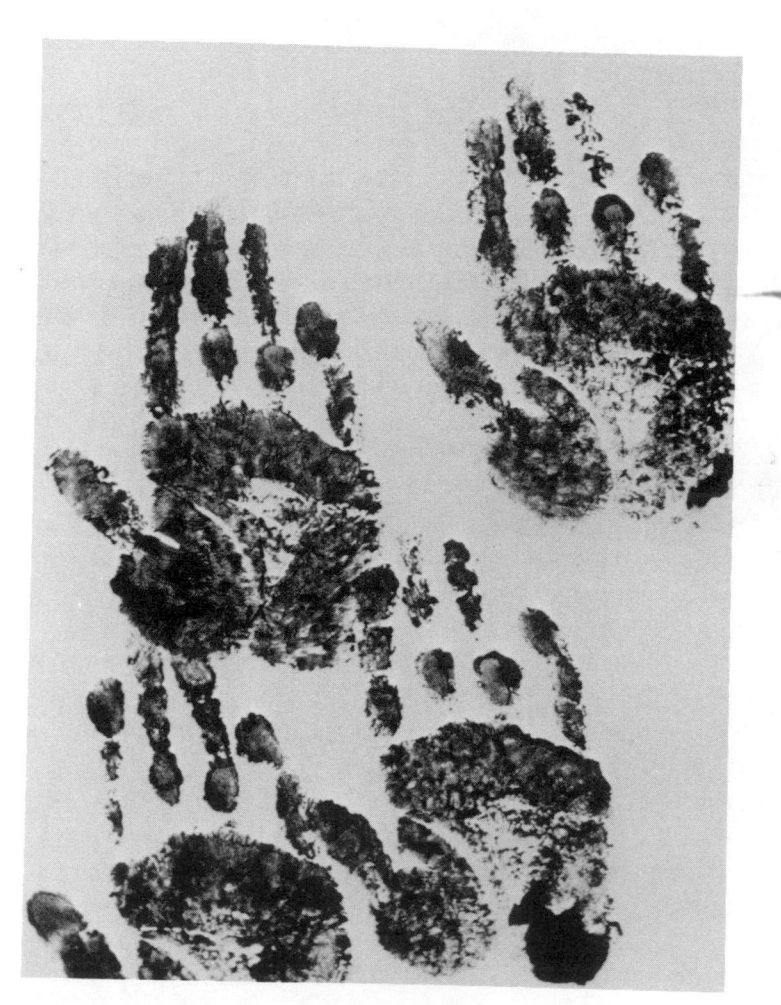

By David, age 4

Handprints

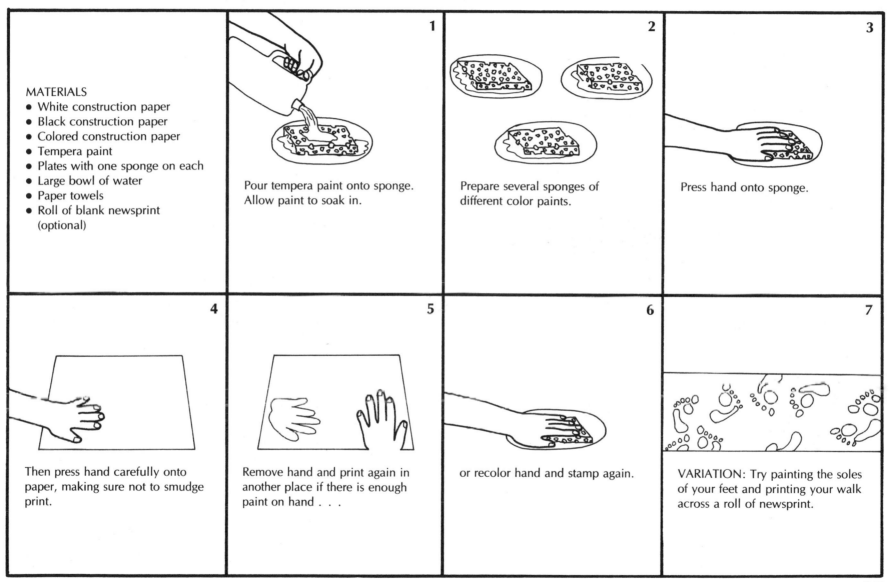

MATERIALS
- White construction paper
- Black construction paper
- Colored construction paper
- Tempera paint
- Plates with one sponge on each
- Large bowl of water
- Paper towels
- Roll of blank newsprint (optional)

1 Pour tempera paint onto sponge. Allow paint to soak in.

2 Prepare several sponges of different color paints.

3 Press hand onto sponge.

4 Then press hand carefully onto paper, making sure not to smudge print.

5 Remove hand and print again in another place if there is enough paint on hand . . .

6 or recolor hand and stamp again.

7 VARIATION: Try painting the soles of your feet and printing your walk across a roll of newsprint.

87

Activity 33 • Vegetable Print

Age Level: Preschool and up

Notes:

- This project can be incorporated into discussions of fall harvest, Thanksgiving, or spring planting.
- Vegetables and fruits may be stamped on large rolls of newsprint to make unique wrapping paper.

- Older children may want to try to create more representational pictures using vegetable and fruit shapes and textures as picture components.

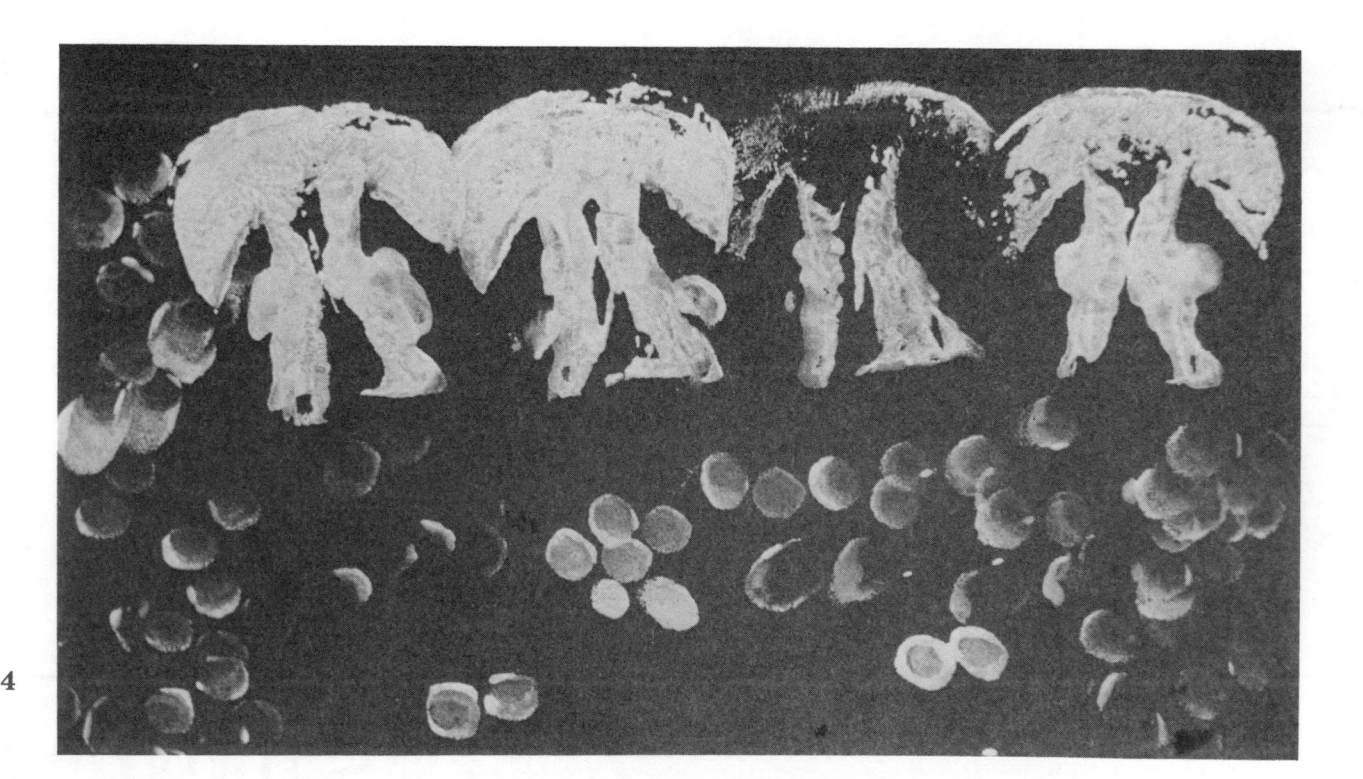

By Kattie, age 4

Vegetable Print

MATERIALS
- A selection of vegetables and fruit, e.g., onions, peppers, mushrooms, celery, carrots, apples, oranges
- Knife
- Shallow dishes
- Sponges
- Tempera paint
- Construction paper

OPTIONAL
- Food coloring
- Colored inks
- Paint brushes
- Baby food jars

1

Place one sponge in each dish.

2

Pour tempera paint onto a sponge and allow it to soak in.

3

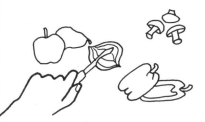

Cut vegetables or fruit into halves.

4

Press flat side of cut vegetable or fruit onto paint-soaked sponge.

5

Then stamp it carefully onto paper, making sure the design does not smudge. If vegetable is still coated, stamp again.

6

Repeat process, using same type of vegetable in another color or using different vegetable in same color. Make design of several stampings.

7

Vegetable and fruit painting may also be done by painting food coloring or colored inks onto flat side with a brush and then stamping.

Age Level: Preschool and up

Notes:

- The sponge shapes should be cut ahead of time by adults for young children.

- For a project variation, try pressing a sponge into white glue, then pressing the sponge onto the paper. Sprinkle glitter over the wet glue, shaking off any excess sprinkles when glue has dried.

- Instead of using glitter as described above, sprinkle soap flakes on top of the glue print to create a snow-like effect.

- You can also try pressing a glue-sponge onto paper and letting the glue design dry. Then apply watercolors as in Activity 26, "White Glue Resist."

- Sponge prints are easy and fun to make, and can be used for simple holiday cards or for making wrapping paper on newsprint or tissue paper.

By Alexis, age 8

Sponge Print

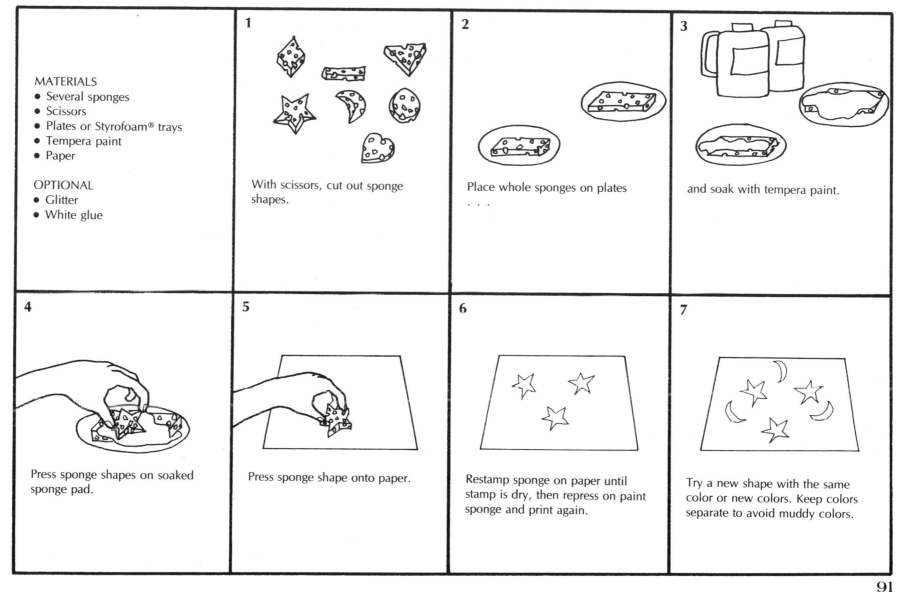

MATERIALS
- Several sponges
- Scissors
- Plates or Styrofoam® trays
- Tempera paint
- Paper

OPTIONAL
- Glitter
- White glue

1 With scissors, cut out sponge shapes.

2 Place whole sponges on plates . . .

3 and soak with tempera paint.

4 Press sponge shapes on soaked sponge pad.

5 Press sponge shape onto paper.

6 Restamp sponge on paper until stamp is dry, then repress on paint sponge and print again.

7 Try a new shape with the same color or new colors. Keep colors separate to avoid muddy colors.

Activity 35 • Sponge Print and Chalk

Age Level: Preschool and up

Notes:

- Sponge prints and chalk offer an interesting range of textures and design possibilities. Make sure children have tried both simple chalk drawing and simple sponge printing before combining these techniques.

- Try doing sponge prints first and then drawing with colored chalk.

- Try adding yet another dimension by creating with watercolor and chalk (see Activity 12), and then adding sponge prints on top of that.

By Sarah, age 9

Sponge Print and Chalk

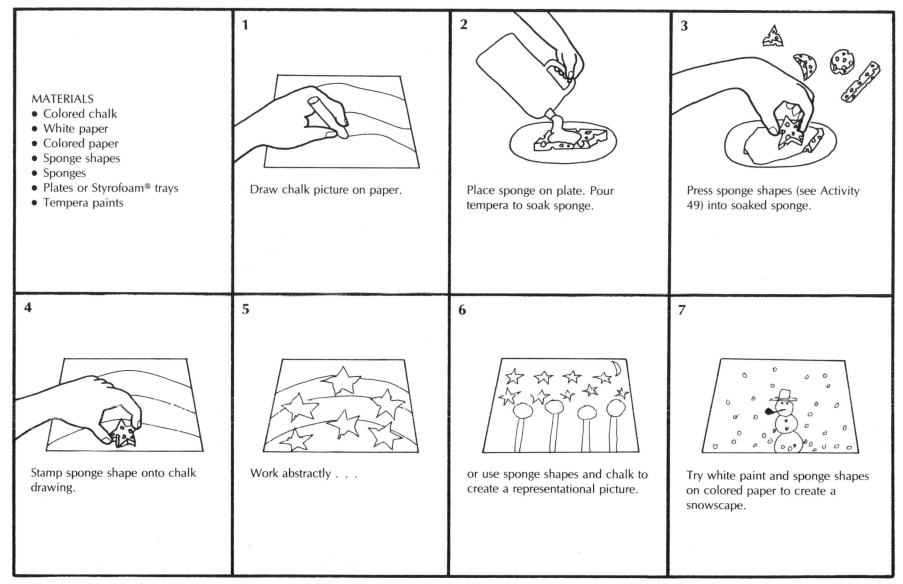

MATERIALS
- Colored chalk
- White paper
- Colored paper
- Sponge shapes
- Sponges
- Plates or Styrofoam® trays
- Tempera paints

1 Draw chalk picture on paper.

2 Place sponge on plate. Pour tempera to soak sponge.

3 Press sponge shapes (see Activity 49) into soaked sponge.

4 Stamp sponge shape onto chalk drawing.

5 Work abstractly . . .

6 or use sponge shapes and chalk to create a representational picture.

7 Try white paint and sponge shapes on colored paper to create a snowscape.

93

Activity 36 • Potato Print

Age Level: Preschool and up

Notes:

- Try different color paints on different colors of paper. Encourage children to keep potato stamps in one color paint to avoid muddying colors. To change colors, the stamp may be washed and dried before reusing.
- Try making potato print cards or wrapping paper on blank newsprint or tissue paper.

- Try pressing a potato stamp into an old ink pad for a softer effect. This process is quite a bit neater as well.

- Try potato printing on top of a dry watercolor painting.

- IMPORTANT: An adult should *always* carve the potato, although children can enjoy designing each stamp.

By Alexis, age 8

Potato Print

MATERIALS
- White potatoes
- Pencil
- Artist's knife
- Tempera paint
- Sponges
- Plates or Styrofoam® trays
- White paper
- Colored paper
- Newsprint
- Tissue paper

CAUTION: Knife to be used *only* by an adult.

1 Cut white potato in half.

2 With pencil, draw design on potato half.

3 Carve negative or positive shape with artist's knife.

4 Place moistened sponge on plate and soak with tempera paint.

5 Press potato into sponge.

6 Stamp potato onto paper.

7 Repeat process several times with one or more stamp designs.

Activity 37 • Stencil Print

Age Level: Preschool and up

Notes:

- Stenciling has recently become a popular decorative art. Older children may want to design their own stencil plates. Materials may usually be found in craft shops or hobby stores. These stencils may be used on cloth as well as on paper.

- Have children stencil across long strips of paper and hang these strips in the classroom as a decorative border.

- Try stenciling a series of cards, or cloth items such as pillows and book bags.

Clockwise from top right; by Tamsen, age 3; Chris, age 4; Kristen, age 3; and Greg, age 4

Stencil Print

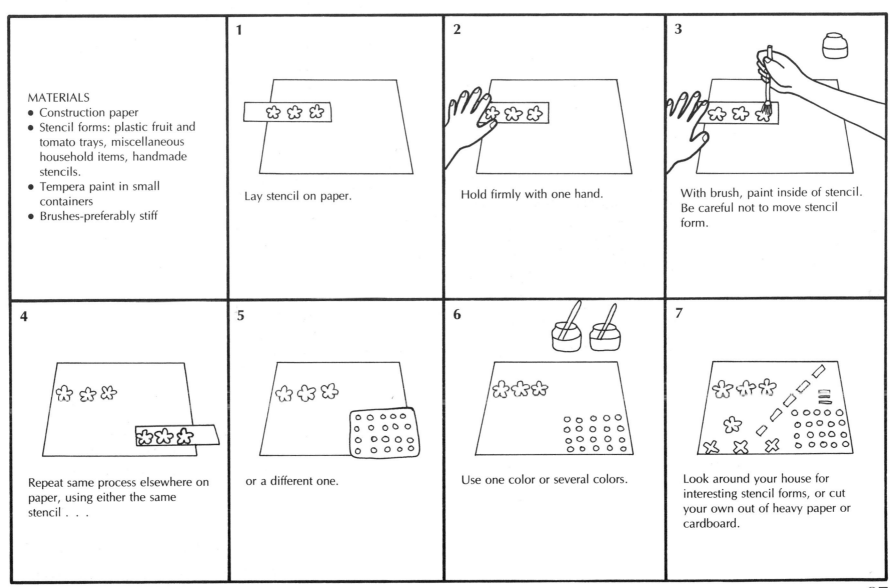

MATERIALS
- Construction paper
- Stencil forms: plastic fruit and tomato trays, miscellaneous household items, handmade stencils.
- Tempera paint in small containers
- Brushes-preferably stiff

1 Lay stencil on paper.

2 Hold firmly with one hand.

3 With brush, paint inside of stencil. Be careful not to move stencil form.

4 Repeat same process elsewhere on paper, using either the same stencil . . .

5 or a different one.

6 Use one color or several colors.

7 Look around your house for interesting stencil forms, or cut your own out of heavy paper or cardboard.

Activity 38 • Blotter Print

Age Level: Preschool and up

Notes:

- This is one of the simplest forms of printing and is easily understood by young children. It also introduces the concept of using a mirror image to create an interesting pattern or design. As an experiment, try placing a small mirror on the edge of a child's picture or design. Ask him/her what has happened to the image.

- Have children play a game of making blotter prints and sharing what the picture reminds them of. Have kids write a story based on their imagination.

By Nathan, age 4

Blotter Print

MATERIALS
- White paper of various textures
- Watercolors
- Watercolor brushes
- Glass of water
- Paper towels

OPTIONAL
- Colored construction paper
- Tempera paints

1

Fold piece of paper in half and then reopen so that paper lies flat.

2

On one side of paper, brush on watercolors to form a design.

3

Fold paper in half along the fold line.

4

Rub hands over surface of folded paper to print design.

5

Carefully reopen.

6

Lay flat to dry.

7

VARIATION
Try using black tempera paint on white paper or white tempera on black paper,

or

try using tempera paint on colored construction paper.

Activity 39 • Etched Monoprint

Age Level: Preschool and up

Notes:

- Try a series of monoprint projects to give children an idea of variations and possibilities within a similar technique.
- This project can be done on a Plexiglas® plate rather than on a tabletop. (See Activity 41, "Colored Monoprint II.")

By Jimmy, age 4

Etched Monoprint

MATERIALS
- Plastic-coated tabletop or piece of Plexiglas®
- Masking tape
- Thick tempera, fingerpaint, or water-soluble printer's ink
- Margarine tub
- Plastic spoon
- Rubber brayer
- Pencil with eraser tip
- Construction paper

1 Lay paper on table. Make a frame around it with masking tape. Be sure not to tape paper to table. Remove paper from frame.

2 Drop a spoonful of paint inside frame. Roll it out with rubber brayer until paint covers the entire inner rectangle.

3 Draw a design on coated surface with a pencil eraser.

4 When picture is complete, carefully place white paper inside taped frame.

5 While holding paper still with one hand, use flat of other hand or fingertips to rub the entire back of paper.

6 Carefully peel paper off table. Lay flat to dry.

7 Try using other tools to make designs in paint: forks, combs, cotton swabs, fingers, etc.

Prints look best when colors of paper and paint are in strong contrast.

Activity 40 • Colored Monoprint I

Age Level: Preschool and up

Notes:

- Do colored monoprints in a series. Ask children how are they the same. How are they different? What different effects can you get from each technique?

- Monoprints have an aspect of magic to them, especially because of the disappearance of the printing "plate." Explore this project in combination with its variations in Activities 41 and 42.

By Beth, age 4

Colored Monoprint I

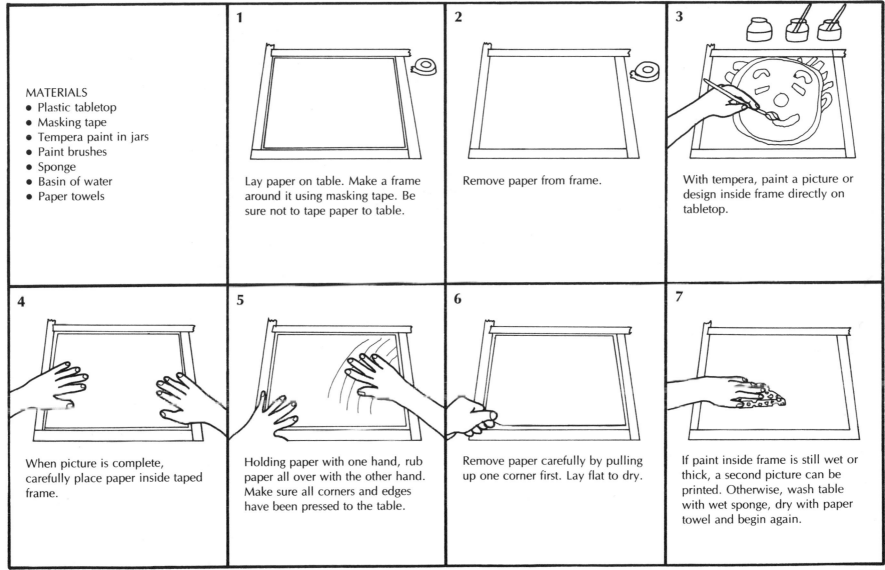

MATERIALS
- Plastic tabletop
- Masking tape
- Tempera paint in jars
- Paint brushes
- Sponge
- Basin of water
- Paper towels

1 Lay paper on table. Make a frame around it using masking tape. Be sure not to tape paper to table.

2 Remove paper from frame.

3 With tempera, paint a picture or design inside frame directly on tabletop.

4 When picture is complete, carefully place paper inside taped frame.

5 Holding paper with one hand, rub paper all over with the other hand. Make sure all corners and edges have been pressed to the table.

6 Remove paper carefully by pulling up one corner first. Lay flat to dry.

7 If paint inside frame is still wet or thick, a second picture can be printed. Otherwise, wash table with wet sponge, dry with paper towel and begin again.

Activity 41 • Colored Monoprint II
Age Level: Preschool and up

Notes:

- For variety, you might want to have children squeeze several colors of ink directly onto the tabletop and roll out a design with the rubber brayer. Then print.

- If a plastic tabletop is not available, see Activity 42 for a variation using Plexiglas® plates to create printing design.

- For younger children especially, this project may be attempted by painting thick tempera designs with a brush directly onto the tabletop surface.

By Shana, age 3

Colored Monoprint II

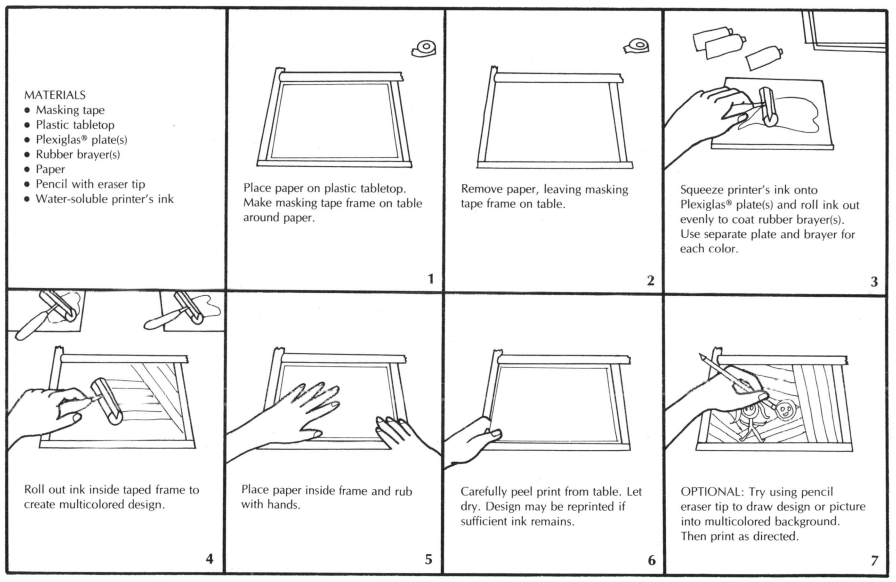

MATERIALS
- Masking tape
- Plastic tabletop
- Plexiglas® plate(s)
- Rubber brayer(s)
- Paper
- Pencil with eraser tip
- Water-soluble printer's ink

1 Place paper on plastic tabletop. Make masking tape frame on table around paper.

2 Remove paper, leaving masking tape frame on table.

3 Squeeze printer's ink onto Plexiglas® plate(s) and roll ink out evenly to coat rubber brayer(s). Use separate plate and brayer for each color.

4 Roll out ink inside taped frame to create multicolored design.

5 Place paper inside frame and rub with hands.

6 Carefully peel print from table. Let dry. Design may be reprinted if sufficient ink remains.

7 OPTIONAL: Try using pencil eraser tip to draw design or picture into multicolored background. Then print as directed.

Activity 42 • Colored Monoprint III

Age Level: Preschool and up

Notes:

- A variation of this project can be done by taping a printing frame on a plastic tabletop, then rolling ink inside of taped frame to create the printing design. (See Activity 41.)

- For younger children especially, this project may be attempted by painting a design with thick tempera paint directly onto the Plexiglas® plate.

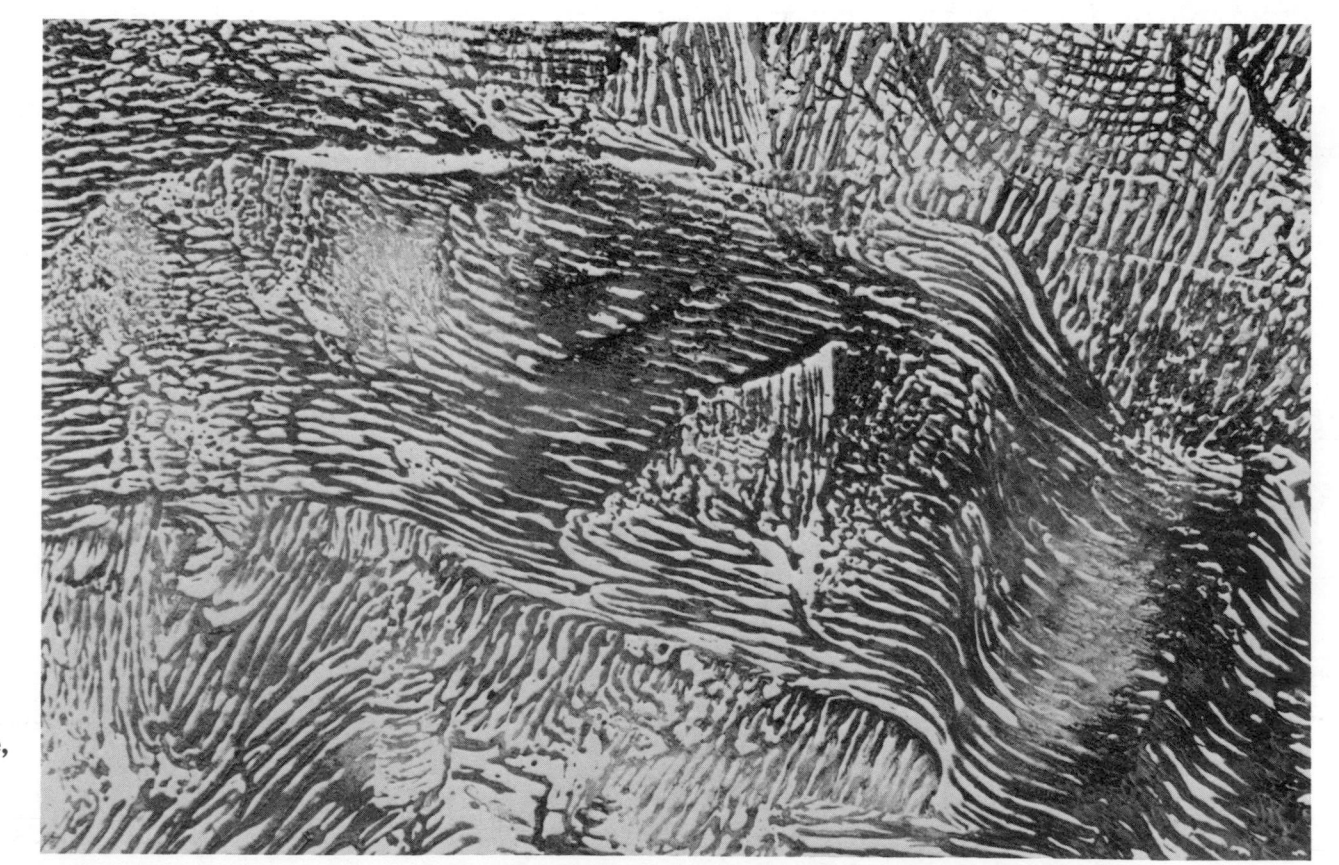

By Christine, age 7

Colored Monoprint III

MATERIALS
- Plexiglas® plate
- Water-soluble printer's ink
- Rubber brayer
- Paper
- Pencil with eraser tip

OPTIONAL
- Printing press

1 Squeeze several colors of printer's ink onto Plexiglas® plate.

2 Roll ink out to make multicolored design.

3 Place paper carefully over plate.

4 Rub with hands or crank through a printing press.

5 Carefully peel off print from plate. Let dry.

6 Reprint plate immediately if sufficient ink remains.

7 OPTIONAL: Draw design with pencil eraser tip after ink has been rolled onto plate. Then print design.

Activity 43 • Styrofoam® Block Print

Age Level: Preschool and up

Notes:

- This simple "block print" technique is very manageable even by the youngest child. A sheet of Styrofoam® punched with pencil-point holes can become an effective print when rolled with more than one color.

- Have children design cards and print them in a series. This makes a nice holiday project.

- This activity may also be done using water-soluble printer's ink that comes in a squeeze tube. Using printers' ink is preferable for older children because it is thicker and less runny than tempera paint.

By Jason, age 11

Styrofoam® Block Print

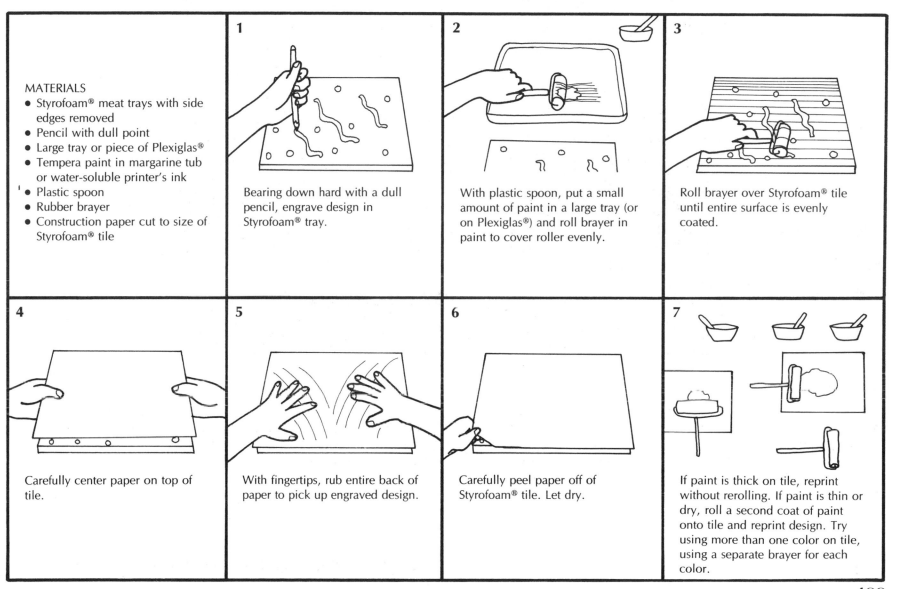

MATERIALS
- Styrofoam® meat trays with side edges removed
- Pencil with dull point
- Large tray or piece of Plexiglas®
- Tempera paint in margarine tub or water-soluble printer's ink
- Plastic spoon
- Rubber brayer
- Construction paper cut to size of Styrofoam® tile

1 Bearing down hard with a dull pencil, engrave design in Styrofoam® tray.

2 With plastic spoon, put a small amount of paint in a large tray (or on Plexiglas®) and roll brayer in paint to cover roller evenly.

3 Roll brayer over Styrofoam® tile until entire surface is evenly coated.

4 Carefully center paper on top of tile.

5 With fingertips, rub entire back of paper to pick up engraved design.

6 Carefully peel paper off of Styrofoam® tile. Let dry.

7 If paint is thick on tile, reprint without rerolling. If paint is thin or dry, roll a second coat of paint onto tile and reprint design. Try using more than one color on tile, using a separate brayer for each color.

Activity 44 • White Glue Print

Age Level: Preschool and up

Notes:

- This is a two-session project because of the time required for the glue to dry.
- This project is simple enough to be managed by very young children. However, these prints will not begin to take on recognizable form until children are in kindergarten or first grade.
- This process is simple and exciting. Children can enjoy making a series of prints, a set of cards, or postcards.
- Older children may want to draw their design first with pencil, and then go over their pencil lines with glue.

By Misa, age 6

White Glue Print

MATERIALS
- White glue in squeeze bottle
- Cardboard or mat board
- Water-soluble printer's ink
- Rubber brayer
- Plexiglas® plate
- Paper

OPTIONAL
- Printing press

1

To prepare printing plate, draw a glue design on cardboard using white glue in a squeeze bottle.

2

Allow to dry thoroughly.

3

Squeeze printer's ink onto Plexiglas® plate.

4

Roll out ink with rubber brayer until brayer is evenly coated.

5

Roll inked brayer over white glue printing plate.

6

Carefully place paper on inked plate and rub with hands, or crank through a printing press.

7

Peel off print and let dry. Reapply ink and print again.

Activity 45 • Masking Tape Print

Age Level: Preschool and up

Notes:

- This project can be done by children of all ages. Preschoolers will enjoy making random designs and building up a layer of tape, while older children can create elaborate representational or abstract designs.

- Older children may want to sketch a design or representational picture before applying the masking tape.

- The tape may be crinkled to create a look of texture.

By Alexis, age 8

Masking Tape Print

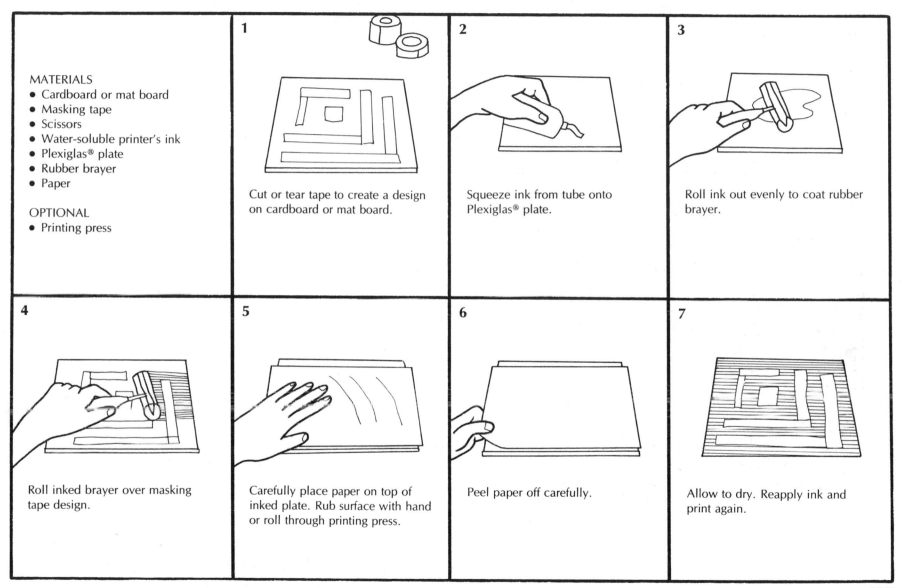

MATERIALS
- Cardboard or mat board
- Masking tape
- Scissors
- Water-soluble printer's ink
- Plexiglas® plate
- Rubber brayer
- Paper

OPTIONAL
- Printing press

1 Cut or tear tape to create a design on cardboard or mat board.

2 Squeeze ink from tube onto Plexiglas® plate.

3 Roll ink out evenly to coat rubber brayer.

4 Roll inked brayer over masking tape design.

5 Carefully place paper on top of inked plate. Rub surface with hand or roll through printing press.

6 Peel paper off carefully.

7 Allow to dry. Reapply ink and print again.

Activity 46 • Cardboard Shapes Print

Age Level: First grade and up

Notes:

- Children may need help cutting out the shapes, but can certainly design their own shapes and relief plate. Posterboard may be substituted for younger children to make cutting easier.

- A similar project may be done by cutting out Styrofoam® shapes and gluing them onto cardboard or Styrofoam® sheets. These shapes are easier to cut.

- Make sure the glued shapes are sufficiently adhered before beginning the printing process.

- Try making holiday cards by printing designs on colored paper with appropriate colors of ink.

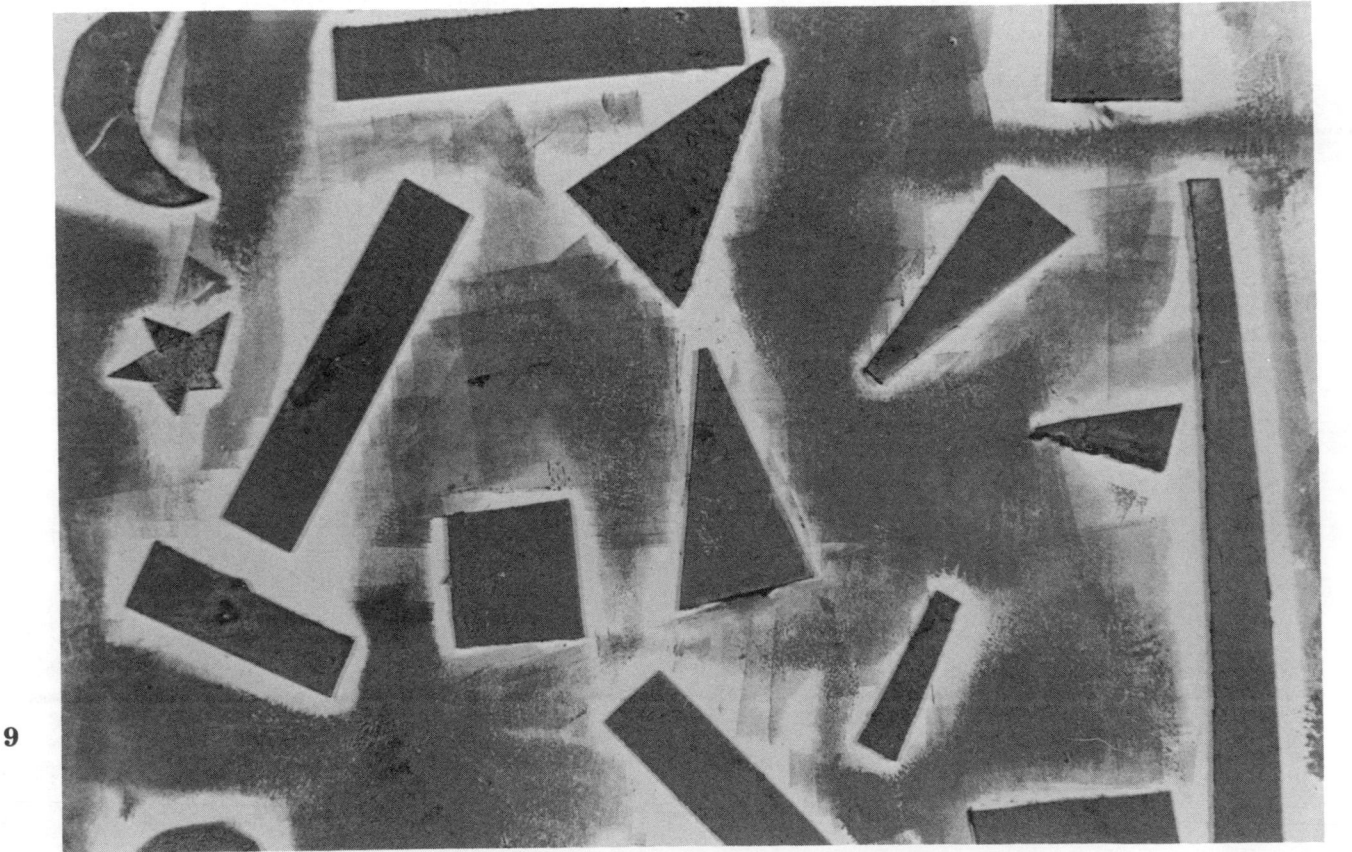

By Emily, age 9

Cardboard Shapes Print

MATERIALS
- Cardboard or mat board
- Scissors
- White glue or rubber cement
- Water-soluble printer's ink
- Rubber brayer
- Plexiglas® plate
- Paper

OPTIONAL
- Printing press

1

Cut out cardboard shapes with scissors.

2

Create design on cardboard surface by gluing on shapes.

3

Squeeze ink onto Plexiglas® plate.

4

Roll ink out evenly to coat rubber brayer.

5

Roll ink over surface of cardboard relief plate.

6

Carefully place paper on inked plate and rub with hands, or crank through a printing press.

7

Peel off print and let dry. Reapply ink and print again.

Activity 47 • Doily Print

Age Level: First grade and up

Notes:

- For a shorter drying time, use rubber cement. White glue will hold better, but needs a longer drying time, so plan accordingly.

- Other types of torn papers or tapes may be added to this process to create a more varied effect.
- Try using more than one color printed on white paper, or use white ink printed on black or colored paper.
- These prints could be tied in with a Valentine's Day activity.

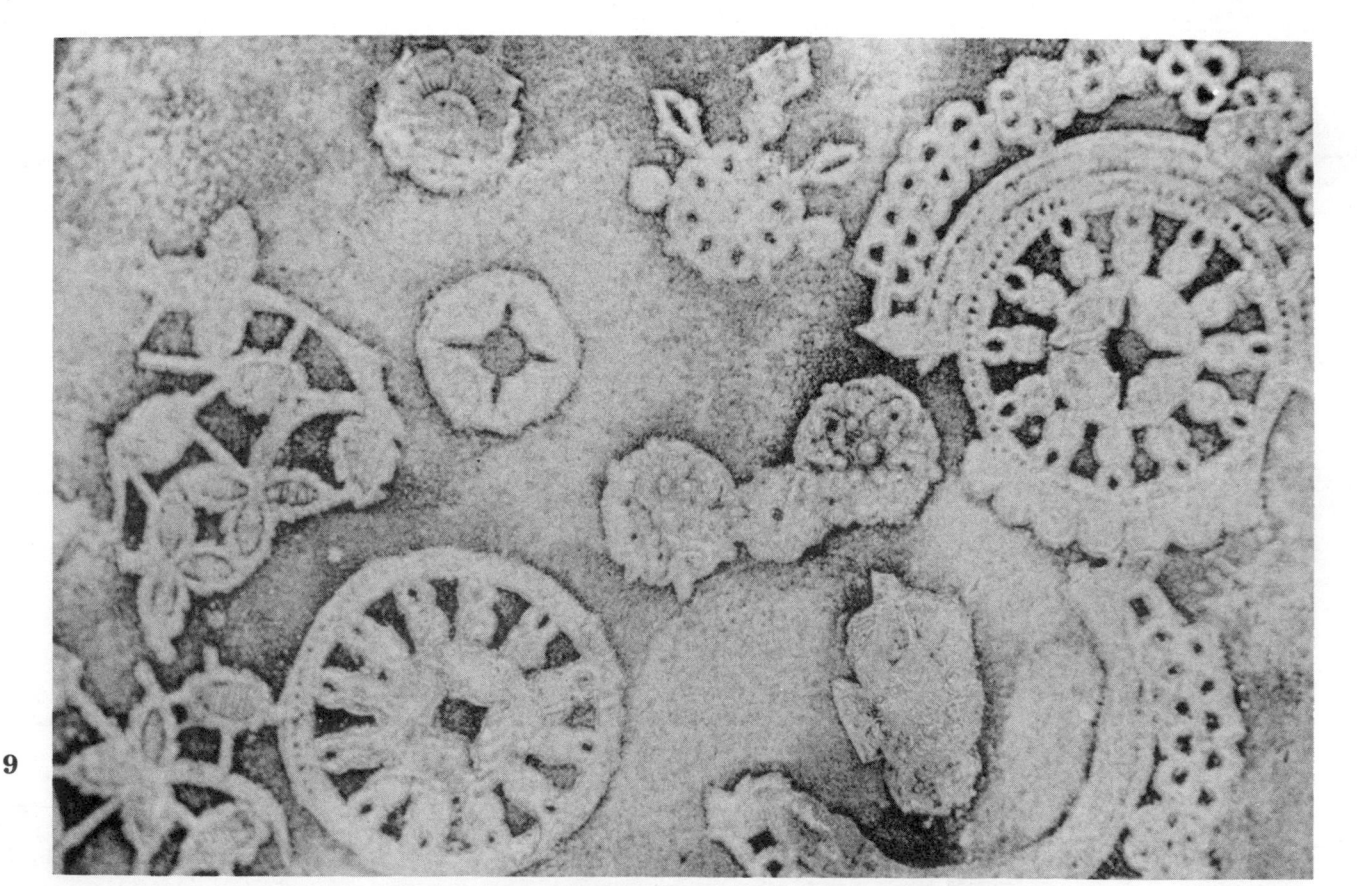

By Emily, age 9

Doily Print

MATERIALS
- Doilies
- Cardboard or mat board
- White glue or rubber cement
- Water-soluble printer's ink
- Rubber brayer
- Plexiglas® plate
- Paper

OPTIONAL
- Scissors
- Printing press

1 Cut or tear doilies and glue onto cardboard plate to create design. Let dry.

2 Squeeze ink onto Plexiglas® plate . . .

3 and roll out evenly with brayer.

4 Roll inked brayer onto doily plate.

5 Carefully place paper on top of plate and rub with hands . . .

6 or crank through a printing press.

7 Peel print from plate and let dry. Reapply ink and print again.

Activity 48 • Texture Print

Age Level: First grade and up

Notes:

- Try creating a design of random textures or try designing a representational picture using various textures and shapes.

- Once a satisfactory design is created, try making prints on several different colors of paper.
- Make a patchwork picture by arranging different colored prints in a patchwork design.

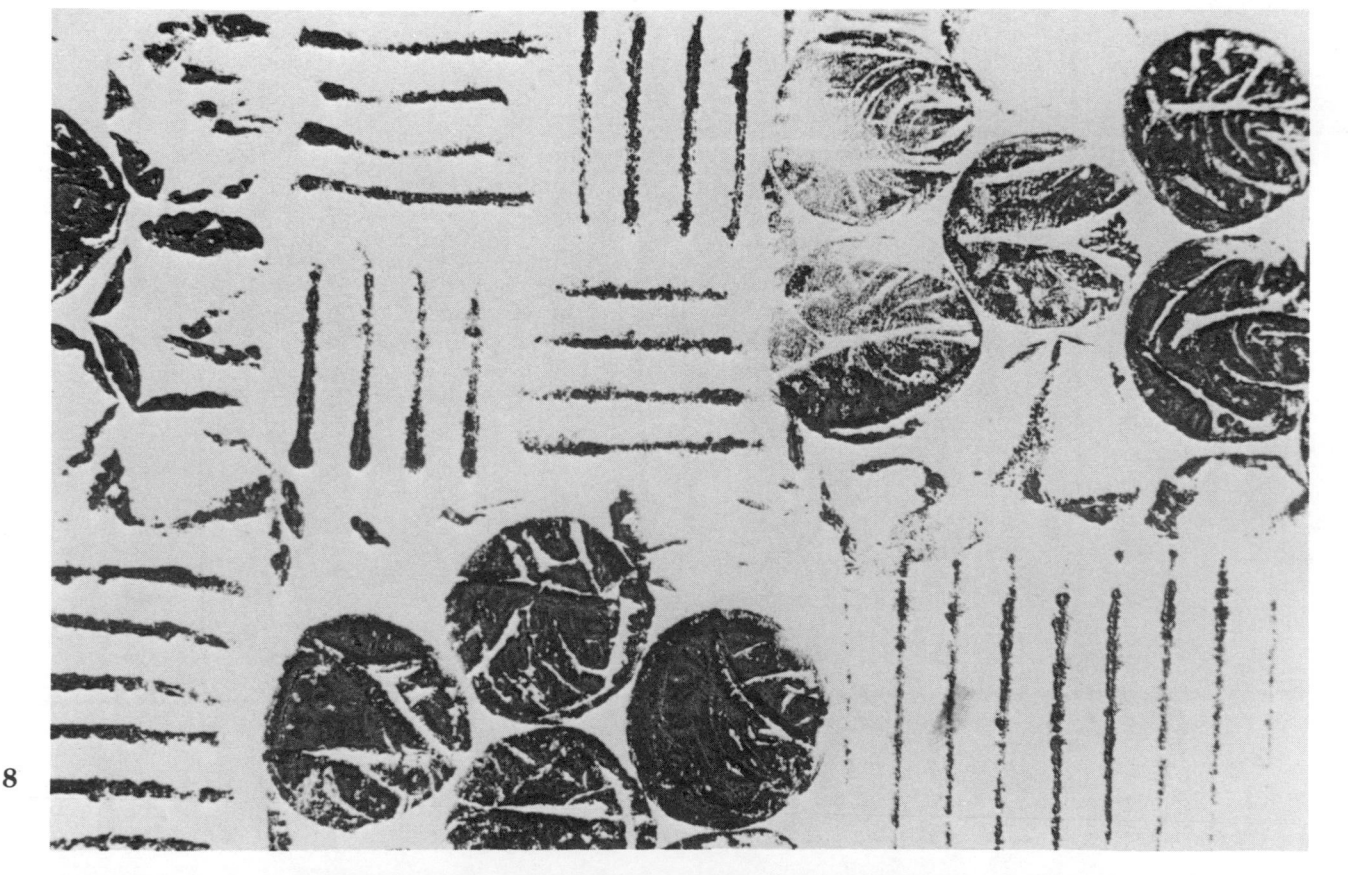

By Alexis, age 8

Texture Print

MATERIALS
- Flat round objects or textures, e.g., toothpicks, bandaids, doilies, sandpaper, aluminum foil, packing plastic, masking tape, etc.
- Cardboard or mat board
- White glue or rubber cement
- Scissors
- Water-soluble printer's ink
- Rubber brayer
- Plexiglas® plate
- Paper

OPTIONAL
- Printing press

1 Glue objects or texture shapes onto cardboard plate to create design. Let dry.

2 Squeeze ink onto Plexiglas® plate . . .

3 and roll out evenly with rubber brayer.

4 Roll inked brayer onto textured printer's plate.

5 Carefully place paper on top of plate and rub with hands, or crank through printing press.

6 Peel print from plate and let dry. Reapply ink and print again.

7 Experiment with many different objects and textures. Choose the most successful ones to use on a final plate design.

Activity 49 • Rubber Stamp Print

Age Level: Kindergarten and up

Notes:

- CAUTION: An adult should always carve the erasers because an artist's knife is very sharp.
- Self-portraits are a favorite subject for young children. A great class project is to have each child design his or her own self-portrait stamp. The class can then create a class picture either on plain paper or on a prepared picture, such as a scene painted with watercolors and washes.
- Create a class mural and written story together as a group project. Use stamps to represent characters in the story.

By Misa, age 6

Rubber Stamp Print

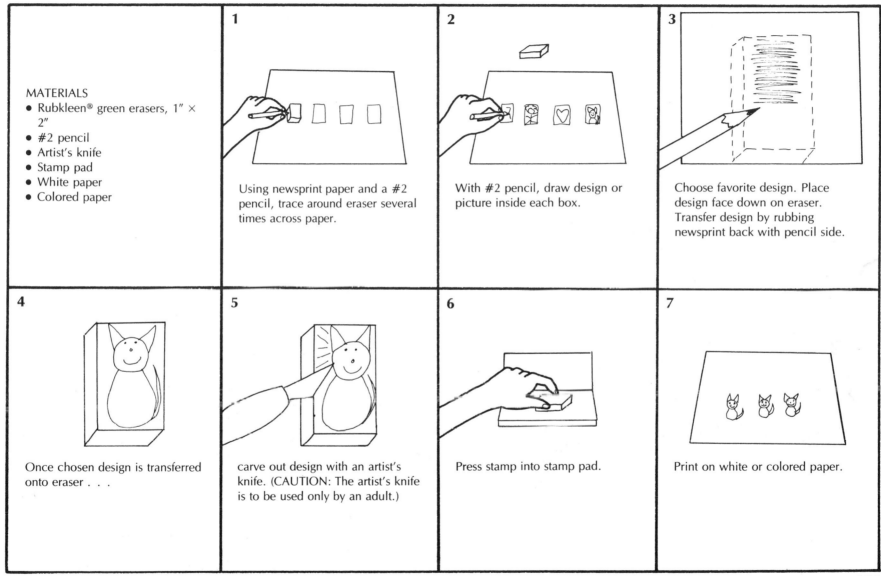

MATERIALS
- Rubkleen® green erasers, 1" × 2"
- #2 pencil
- Artist's knife
- Stamp pad
- White paper
- Colored paper

1 Using newsprint paper and a #2 pencil, trace around eraser several times across paper.

2 With #2 pencil, draw design or picture inside each box.

3 Choose favorite design. Place design face down on eraser. Transfer design by rubbing newsprint back with pencil side.

4 Once chosen design is transferred onto eraser . . .

5 carve out design with an artist's knife. (CAUTION: The artist's knife is to be used only by an adult.)

6 Press stamp into stamp pad.

7 Print on white or colored paper.

COLLAGE AND RELIEF

Collage and relief form a bridge between two-dimensional and three-dimensional art. Collage involves the application of materials and flat objects to a two-dimensional surface. In relief, these materials begin to project out of the flat plane into the third dimension.

Although work in collage and relief is still basically two-dimensional, it begins to bulge at the surface. Colors and textures push their way out of the smooth, flat page as a variety of shapes and images burst forth from the two-dimensional plane. The young child delights in exploring textures in very tactile ways as his or her natural relish for touching things takes hold.

Notes on Jenny:
The Song of the Artist

Jenny sits at a table covered with yarns, cloth scraps, buttons, and wooden knobs. As she works on her collage, Jenny babbles to herself. Her words, an integral part of her process, compose a merry sing-song punctuated with squeals of delight, sighs of frustration, gurgles of glee, swinging of arms, and tossing of head. Her animated song goes like this:

I'm going to make a LITtle perSON.
'cause I'm a LITtle perSON.
and I have BLUE EYES!
OH! There's some blue eyes.
They're SMOOTH . . . and SHINY!

They can ROLL . . . ROLL . . . ROLL across my cheek.
OH! This glue is GOOOO-EEYYYY!
It's sticking to my FIN-GERS!
Now I need a mouth . . .
There's one . . . and legs too!
I'm making LITtle LEGS, LIKE MEEEE! . . .
'cause I have LITtle LEGS.
I CAN DANCE, DANCE, DANCE . . . ROUND AND ROUND!
This time I'm not going to use a lot of glue
'cause it will
DRIP
DRIP
DRIP
ALL Over the PLACE!
Now I'm going to put hair on.
RED!! I need RREDD! LIKE MEEE!
There's some RED!
SOFT . . . AND CURLY!
So SOFT on my cheek . . .
YUCK !! I got GLUE on me! [giggle]
OOOOOOOOUUUUUUEEEEEEE!!! It's
GOOOOEEEEEYYYYY!!!
THIS GLUE IS GOOEEYYY!
STICKY YARN . . . CURLY YARN . . . HAIRY YARN!
GOOEY YARN!
THERE. IT'S DONE.
IT'S ME!
IT'S MMEEE!
IT FEELS LIKE MMEEEE!!!

Activity 50 • Self-Stick Vinyl Collage

Age Level: Preschool and up

Notes:

- Self-stick vinyl collage is fun for children because it does not require any glue. Young children will need help starting to separate the paper from the backing at one corner, yet they will enjoy peeling the backing off and sticking on their shapes.

- A variety of colors, patterns, and textures of self-stick vinyl are available. Providing a variety of papers, especially ones with different "feels" will contribute to the success of this project.

- These collages may be applied to three-dimensional surfaces such as boxes, cans, and so on.

By Kimberly, age 4

Self-Stick Vinyl Collage

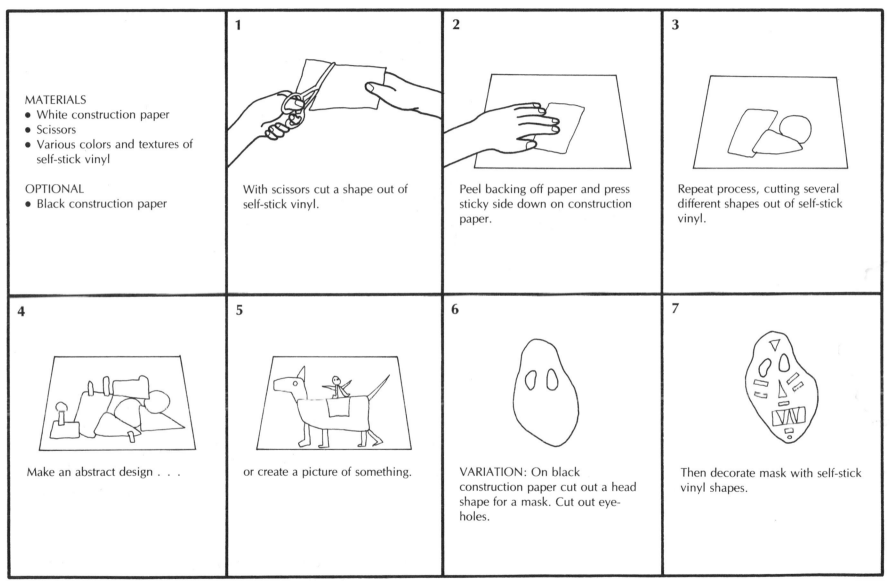

MATERIALS
- White construction paper
- Scissors
- Various colors and textures of self-stick vinyl

OPTIONAL
- Black construction paper

1 With scissors cut a shape out of self-stick vinyl.

2 Peel backing off paper and press sticky side down on construction paper.

3 Repeat process, cutting several different shapes out of self-stick vinyl.

4 Make an abstract design . . .

5 or create a picture of something.

6 VARIATION: On black construction paper cut out a head shape for a mask. Cut out eye-holes.

7 Then decorate mask with self-stick vinyl shapes.

Activity 51 • Tissue Collage

Age Level: Preschool and up

Notes:

- This technique creates quite colorful designs, especially when a shiny finish surface is applied to the finished product.
- Younger children can learn about overlaying colors and making new colors in this way.

- Older children can take this project one step further to create something else with their tissue collage. (See Activity 52, "Tissue Collage Bird Hanging.")
- For a variation, try combining tissue paper with other types of paper, such as grained rice paper or doilies.

By Kristen, age 3

Tissue Collage

MATERIALS
- White glue
- Water
- Baby food jars
- Paint brush
- White or manilla paper
- Brightly colored tissue paper
- Shellac or other shiny finish
- 1" to 2" wide sponge brush

1

In baby food jars, dilute white glue to milky consistency. Make a pile of torn tissue paper.

2

Place a piece of tissue paper on white paper. Brush glue over tissue paper.

3

Continue placing tissue on paper and brushing glue over it.

4

Try to fill entire paper with many colors of tissue paper. Overlap colors.

5

When glue has dried, apply a shiny (glossy) finish to picture with wide sponge brush. NOTE: Extra adult supervision should be given while shellac is in use.

6

VARIATIONS: Before applying finish, draw designs on picture with dark marker . . .

7

or draw a line design on paper first and then apply tissue and glue.

Activity 52 • Tissue Collage Bird Hanging

Age Level: First grade and up

Notes:

- The tissue collage may be sprayed or painted with shellac once dry. (IMPORTANT: To be done only by an adult in a well-ventilated area.) This makes the collage shiny and brightens the colors.

- Older children may want to cut out and decorate other shapes to create a variety of animals or creatures.
- Many birds or animals may be strung together to make a free-hanging mobile.
- Try making a mobile with a theme, such as a trip to the zoo, farm animals, a forest scene, a celestial scene, and so on.

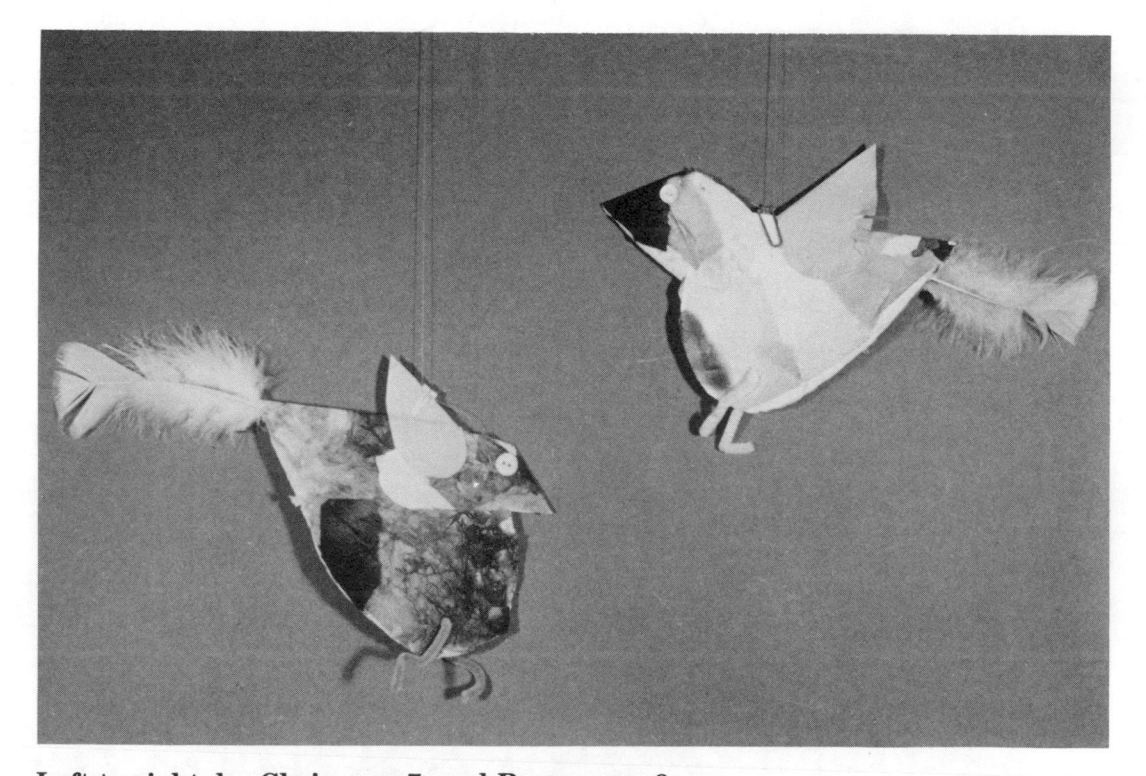

Left to right, by Chris, age 7, and Reena, age 6

Tissue Collage Bird Hanging

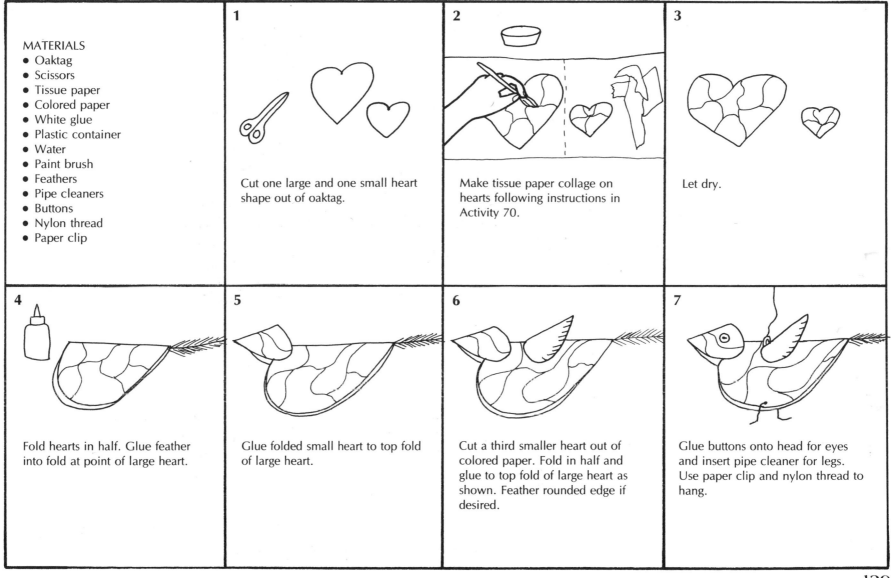

MATERIALS
- Oaktag
- Scissors
- Tissue paper
- Colored paper
- White glue
- Plastic container
- Water
- Paint brush
- Feathers
- Pipe cleaners
- Buttons
- Nylon thread
- Paper clip

1 Cut one large and one small heart shape out of oaktag.

2 Make tissue paper collage on hearts following instructions in Activity 70.

3 Let dry.

4 Fold hearts in half. Glue feather into fold at point of large heart.

5 Glue folded small heart to top fold of large heart.

6 Cut a third smaller heart out of colored paper. Fold in half and glue to top fold of large heart as shown. Feather rounded edge if desired.

7 Glue buttons onto head for eyes and insert pipe cleaner for legs. Use paper clip and nylon thread to hang.

Activity 53 • Fabric Collage

Age Level: Preschool and up

Notes:

- These collages can be as abstract or as representational as each child desires. Either way, combining textures, colors, and prints gives potential for intriguing works of art.

- Encourage older children to work two ways: (1) creating spontaneous fabric collages and (2) sketching out a design or picture beforehand with a plan for use of materials. Let students discover which way is more satisfying for them.

By Aaron, age 4

Fabric Collage

MATERIALS
- Heavy paper or cardboard
- Small pieces of cloth
- Strips of burlap
- White glue in small jar
- Paint brush for glue

1
Paint glue onto back of cloth to be glued.

2
Press piece, glue side down, onto paper.

3
Now paint glue on the back of next collage piece.

4
Repeat process . . .

5
until design or picture is complete.

6
Use a variety of colors and textures to create an abstract design . . .

7
or a representational picture.

Age Level: Preschool and up

Notes:

- This collage is a great introduction to texture. Try experimenting with a "feel box" before doing this project. Cut a hand-size hole in a box and place a number of different textured objects inside. Have children describe each texture and guess what it is.

- For older children, a blindfold walk can also be a fun way to explore texture. Have children pair up, one child blindfolded and the other child acting as "guide." Let the guide walk the blindfolded child around and present him or her with many different textures to feel.

By Robby, age 5

Soft Collage

MATERIALS
- Pieces of soft materials, e.g., foam, carpet, cloth, cotton, yarn, etc.
- White glue in jar
- Brush for glue
- Construction paper or cardboard
- Scissors

1

Cut desired shapes out of materials.

2

Brush white glue on the back of each shape, one at a time . . .

3

and press onto construction paper or cardboard.

4

Build a soft collage that feels good. Make it furry or spongy, silky or stringy.

5

Try making an animal collage . . .

6

or your favorite thing.

7

Try making soft sculptures by decorating three-dimensional objects like cardboard tubes, boxes, balls, etc.

Activity 55 • Eggshell Collage

Age Level: Preschool and up

Notes:

- This makes a great post-Easter project. It is colorful and creates an interesting texture.

- Have the children save their Easter egg shells.
- Try using eggshells in combination with other materials, such as glitter.

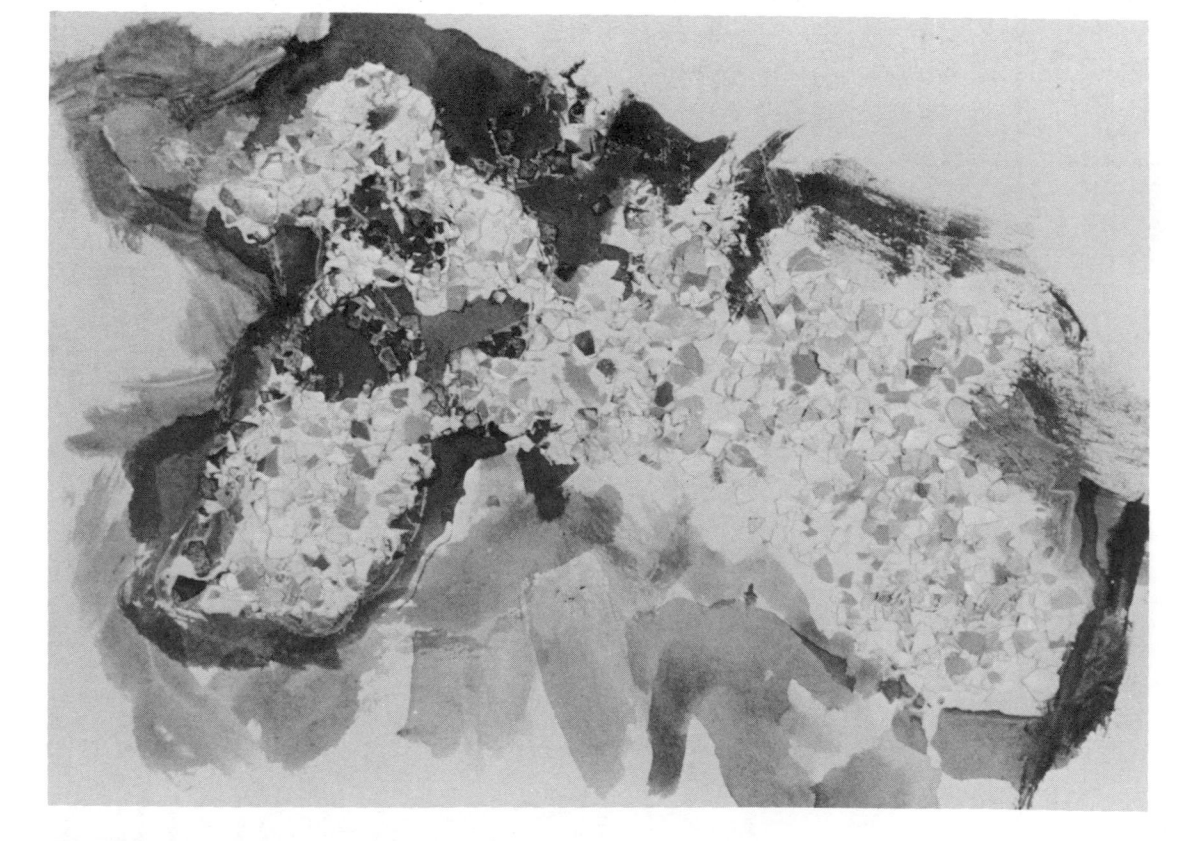

By Rebecca, age 4

Eggshell Collage

MATERIALS
- Colored shells from Easter eggs
- Plastic bag
- Large bowl
- White glue in jar
- Brush for glue
- Watercolors
- Watercolor brush
- Glass of water

OPTIONAL
- Tempera paint
- White egg shells

1 Put eggshells in plastic bag. Pound with fist or heavy object to crush the shells.

2 Pour shell pieces into bowl.

3 Paint glue onto paper where eggshells are to adhere.

4 Sprinkle shells over glued area.

5 Shake loose shells back into bowl. Allow glue to dry.

6 With watercolors, paint a picture around the eggshell design.

7 VARIATION: Glue white eggshells onto paper. When dry, paint shells and paper with tempera or watercolor.

Activity 56 • Stick Mask

Age Level: Preschool and up

Notes:

- Preschool children can easily make a single-faced stick mask. A double-faced mask will require help in joining together the two surfaces.

- Older children can punch holes around the edges of two masks and weave them together with yarn.

- The double-faced mask offers the special opportunity for children to integrate mask-making with storytelling. Each mask side can represent a different character or the same character in a different mood. Older children can create intricate stories with several double-faced masks.

- Using cardboard or oaktag, children can design and cut their own mask shape. They can then trace it and cut a second identical shape for a more elaborate version of the double-faced mask.

By Katy, age 8

Stick Mask

MATERIALS
- Cardboard pizza discs or cut cardboard circles
- 18" long ¼" dowels
- Pencil
- Markers
- Tempera paint
- Brushes
- White glue
- Colored paper
- Masking tape

OPTIONAL
- Glitter
- Yarn
- Notions

1

For a single-faced mask, cut eyes in disc for seeing if desired.

2

Design mask face using markers, paint, glitter, ribbons, etc.

3

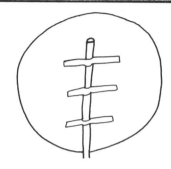

When mask is dry, tape dowel to mask back with dowel extending below mask for holding.

4

For a double-faced mask, repeat steps one and two, making sure that eye holes are cut in exact same place if see-through eyes are desired.

5

Decorate second mask with totally different character.

6

When dry, tape stick to back of one mask, then glue or tape second mask onto backside.

7

Make up a story using your two mask characters. Act it out for a friend.

Activity 57 • Hardware Mask

Age Level: First grade and up

Notes:

- These masks make wonderful wall plaques that are very "real" and substantial. Young children may use glue to adhere hardware to the wood plaque, while older children will enjoy hammering and screwing hardware on. Young children may be presented with this option, however, for many of them will enjoy the opportunity to work with real tools. However, read the following cautions.

- CAUTION: This project is *not* appropriate for young pre-schoolers who are apt to put small pieces of hardware in their mouths.
- CAUTION: Adult supervision is a *must* when children are using tools, particularly with younger children.

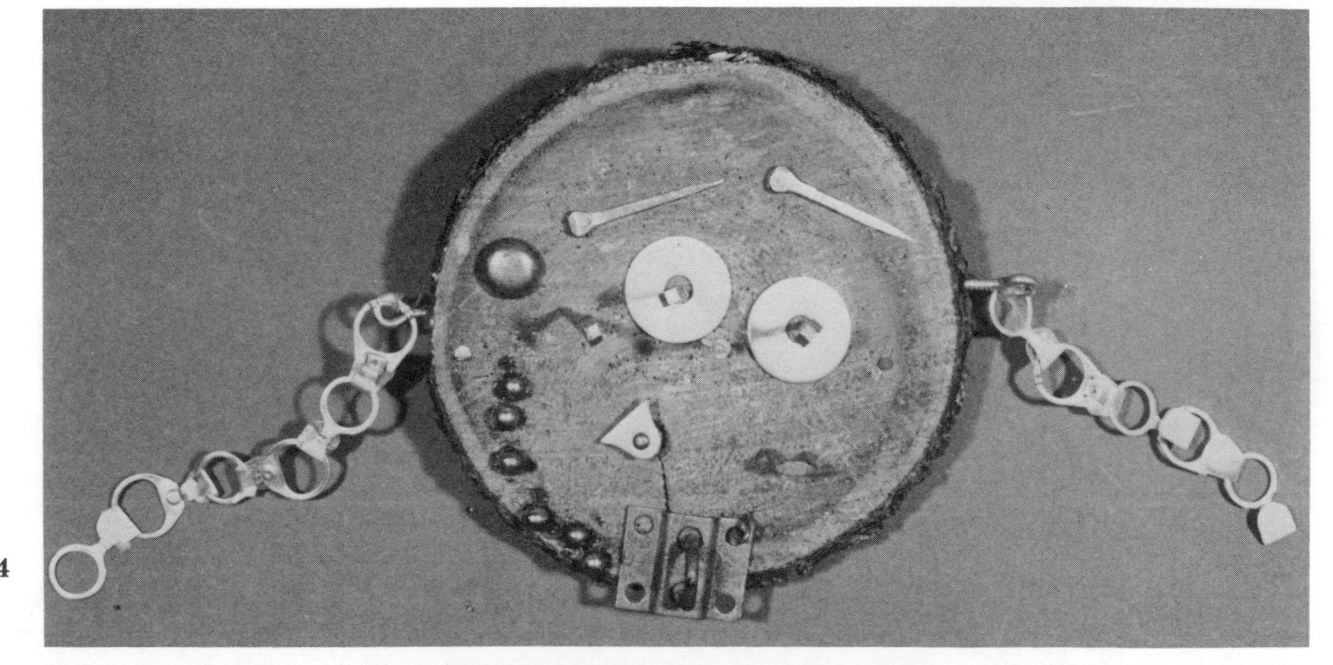

By Kattie, age 4

Hardware Mask

MATERIALS
- Flat slabs of wood or discs from cross-section cut of log
- Assorted hardware including nails, screws, nuts, bolts, washers, etc.
- Hammer
- Screw driver
- White glue in jar
- Small brush for glue
- String
- Screw eyes

CAUTION: Make certain nails, screws, etc., are rust-free and note cautions on previous page.

1

Find pieces of hardware to use as facial features.

2

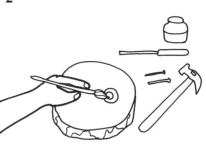

On flat wood surface, glue, hammer, or screw on pieces of hardware.

3

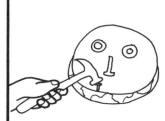

Be certain all pieces are firmly attached.

4

Use other hardware to decorate mask. Depict war paint, freckles, hair, etc.

5

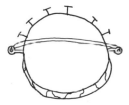

With screw eyes, attach a string to the back for hanging.

6

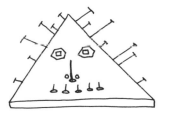

Try making masks on other wooden shapes . . .

7

or make several masks to form a totem pole.

Activity 58 • Papier-Mâché Mask

Age Level: First grade and up

Notes:

- Papier-mâché mixture is made by mixing together flour and water to a batter-like consistency. One-inch strips of newspaper are then dipped into the mixture and applied to the balloon mold. Cover the entire balloon surface. Allow each layer to dry thoroughly before adding the next layer. Layers can be alternated between black-and-white newsprint and colored newsprint to ensure covering the entire balloon surface with each application.

- Papier-mâché pulp is made by shredding newspaper and stirring it into the flour-and-water mixture. Let it sit for several hours or overnight. Then squeeze the mixture through your fingers to make pulp. The pulp may be added to the papier-mâché surface to shape features. Let it dry thoroughly before painting.

- This project is messy so plan accordingly!

- IMPORTANT: An adult must be responsible for cutting the balloon mold in half if a knife is used.

By Misa, age 6

Papier-Mâché Mask

MATERIALS
- Balloons
- Newspaper
- White flour
- Water
- Large mixing bowl
- Long-handled spoon
- Knife
- Scissors
- Tempera paint
- Brushes
- Yarn
- Cloth scraps (optional)
- White glue

1

Blow up balloon to desired mask size.

2

Prepare papier-mâché mixture. Dip 1" newspaper strips into paste, then layer them on balloon surface. Apply 3 layers of strips, allowing each to dry in between.

3

Cut balloon in half, creating two separate mask bases. Cut holes for eyes if desired.

4

Using papier-mâché pulp, build features into mask, including the nose, mouth, ears, eyes, eyebrows, etc. Let dry.

5

Using tempera, paint mask a base color.

6

When dry, paint on features. Yarn and other scraps may be glued onto these masks. Punch holes at sides to tie mask on.

7

Try making a really large mask, or a small, doll-size mask.

Activity 59 • Wooden Shapes Relief

Age Level: Preschool and up

NOTES:

- Older children can extend this project to make "relief people" on scraps of wood or cardboard. These can be displayed on the wall or added to a group-made mural.

- Have children create their own "computer room" or "spaceship' panel" full of knobs and screens. They can use any number of chosen techniques to fill in "television screens." Have them use their creations as a prop. They can write a script and put on a play!

By students of The Children's Garden, a preschool

Wooden Shapes Relief

MATERIALS
- Piece of masonite, or wood slab, plywood, etc.
- Wooden objects such as knobs, spools, blocks, discs, etc.
- White glue in small jar
- Paint brush for glue

OPTIONAL
- Spray paint (to be used *only* by an adult in a well-ventilated area)

1

Paint glue on back of chosen wooden object.

2

Press object onto flat wooden surface.

3

Paint glue on the back of second object . . .

4

and press onto wooden surface.

5

Repeat process until surface is covered with wooden objects.

6

Try gluing wooden pieces onto three-dimensional surfaces like an old bench, step ladder, chair, or stool.

7

Finished product can be left in wood tones or coated with spray paint.

Activity 60 • Rolled Paper Animal Relief

Age Level: Fourth grade and up

Notes:

- This technique is also known as quilling.
- For a challenging class project, create a totally quilled mural in which 100 percent of the surface is covered. Try using different width strips to create more dimension.

- Create an abstract relief design using different width paper strips and different colors to create an undulating surface (visually and actually).

Left to right, by Angela, age 11 and Jenny, age 10

Rolled Paper Animal Relief

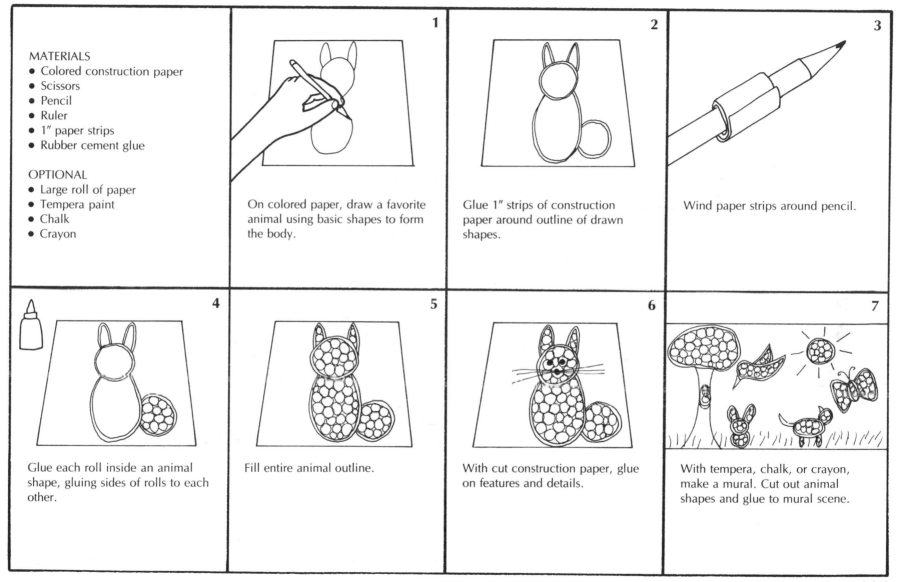

MATERIALS
- Colored construction paper
- Scissors
- Pencil
- Ruler
- 1" paper strips
- Rubber cement glue

OPTIONAL
- Large roll of paper
- Tempera paint
- Chalk
- Crayon

1 On colored paper, draw a favorite animal using basic shapes to form the body.

2 Glue 1" strips of construction paper around outline of drawn shapes.

3 Wind paper strips around pencil.

4 Glue each roll inside an animal shape, gluing sides of rolls to each other.

5 Fill entire animal outline.

6 With cut construction paper, glue on features and details.

7 With tempera, chalk, or crayon, make a mural. Cut out animal shapes and glue to mural scene.

SCULPTURE

No child can resist the tactile experience offered by work in the third dimension. Squeezing, rolling, poking, twisting, stretching—these activities come naturally to kids.

Each of the materials described in this section has a texture and a character of its own and is conducive to making certain kinds of sculpture. It is part of each child's artistic process to discover the properties unique to each material: what clay can do that wax cannot do; what wax can do that sawdust compound cannot do, and so on. Each texture and consistency provides the child with a new tactile experience and a new challenge. Better still, assist the child in making his or her own materials as described in project instructions. This is fun for kids and provides them with added sensory and learning experiences.

When working with modeling compounds, provide children with small "found" items to give them options for adding detail to the work. Pine cone petals, small stones, twigs, and acorn caps are ideal.

In some projects, a stuffed or live animal in view of the working artist can provide inspiration as well as vividness of detail that memory often cannot supply.

Notes on Tasha: Young Sculptor at Work

Tasha, age two and a half, nimbly works her ball of clay. Her fingers, still round with baby fat, pinch and poke the clay assuredly. There is no doubt that Tasha is at home with this medium.

As Tasha works her clay, her eye catches sight of Wurlitzer, her pet dog, who has just wandered into the room. Her clay ball immediately begins to bark and romp. Tasha's intention is clear: to make Wurlitzer her live model.

As the clay ball barks, Tasha tears a piece of clay from its bulk and resets it to form the head on the body. She eyes Wurlitzer, then pulls long ears from the clay head and presses two bits of eyes onto it. Tasha pauses. She gets out of her chair, marches over to Wurlitzer, pats him, converses with him, and strokes his tail before returning to her work. Tasha rolls out a long clay worm and affixes it to the other end of her clay creature. Voila! A tail! The clay dog romps noisily across the tabletop. Wurlitzer wanders back into the other room.

Activity 61 • Clay: Pinch Pot

Age Level: Preschool and up

Notes:

- Clay, a most basic three-dimensional material, is extremely enticing. Once children begin to play with clay, they seem unable to put it down!

- Repeat this project on an ongoing basis, giving children the opportunity to explore and then improve their pinch-pot technique.

- Older children can try mixing different colors of clay (that fire at the same temperature) to create a visual design to the surface of their pots.

- Pinch pots can be a basic starting point from which to create sculptures.

- If you do not have a kiln available, ask a local potter if he or she will fire your pieces.

- A local potter may also provide you with glazes. Otherwise, clay pieces may be painted with acrylic paint after they are fired.

- If you are to have a local potter fire your work, check with him or her beforehand about using a clay appropriate to the firing temperatures the potter usually works with. (Different clays fire at different temperatures.)

- IMPORTANT: If a school kiln is used, it should be used only by an adult.

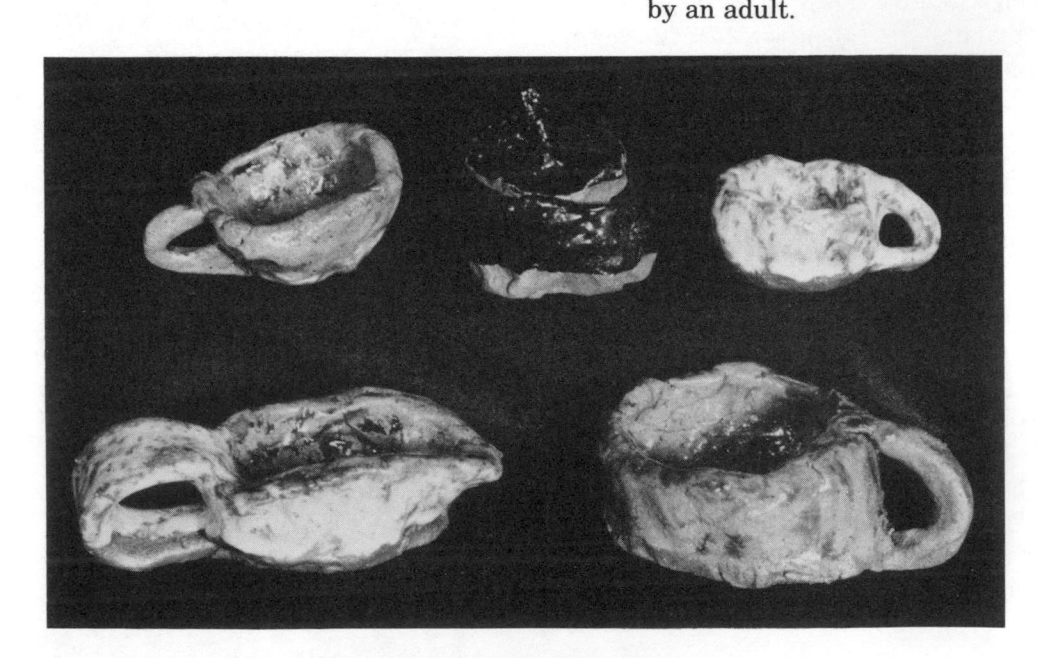

Top, left to right, by Travis, age 4; Robby, age 5; Christopher, age 4. Bottom left, Nathan, age 4; bottom right, anonymous

Clay: Pinch Pot

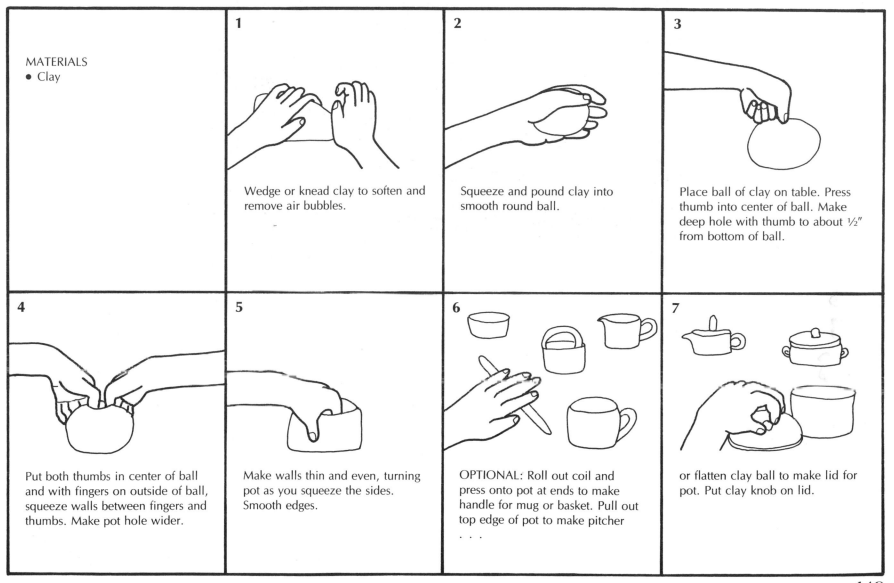

MATERIALS
• Clay

1 Wedge or knead clay to soften and remove air bubbles.

2 Squeeze and pound clay into smooth round ball.

3 Place ball of clay on table. Press thumb into center of ball. Make deep hole with thumb to about ½" from bottom of ball.

4 Put both thumbs in center of ball and with fingers on outside of ball, squeeze walls between fingers and thumbs. Make pot hole wider.

5 Make walls thin and even, turning pot as you squeeze the sides. Smooth edges.

6 OPTIONAL: Roll out coil and press onto pot at ends to make handle for mug or basket. Pull out top edge of pot to make pitcher . . .

7 or flatten clay ball to make lid for pot. Put clay knob on lid.

Age Level: Preschool and up

Notes on Misa: A Love Affair with Clay

It is not until my daughter Misa is nineteen months old that I think to buy her some sticks of colored clay. Misa is delighted with my gift and, after only a moment's hesitation, grabs the clay out of my hands. She pokes and pinches it, pulls and twists it. Though she seems to have little notion of what this strange stuff is, her fingers cannot stop fiddling with it.

I break off some small, manageable pieces for her and put them into a plastic cup. Misa grabs the cup and holds it close to her, pleased. She will not put it down! She insists on taking it everywhere: on car rides, bike rides, and walks through the woods. She clutches it in her fist as she peddles her four-wheeler, listens to stories, and dances to records. She even insists on having it in her lap at dinnertime. When Misa wants to bring it into the tub, I decide that things are getting out of hand. I try to hide it; my trick doesn't work. Finally, we compromise, and put the clay in a cup in the soap tray. I am surprised and relieved when Misa willingly parts with her clay at bedtime. I am less surprised to hear her "eh-eh-ing" for her clay at 5:30 the next morning, hands outstretched.

Misa plays with her clay day after day. She learns to roll it into balls, make worms, flatten pancakes, and cut it with a wooden knife, all in a very short time. The more she works with the clay, the stronger her fingers become and the more adept she becomes at making shapes. The more adept she gets, the stronger her attachment to the clay becomes. Misa has found her medium!

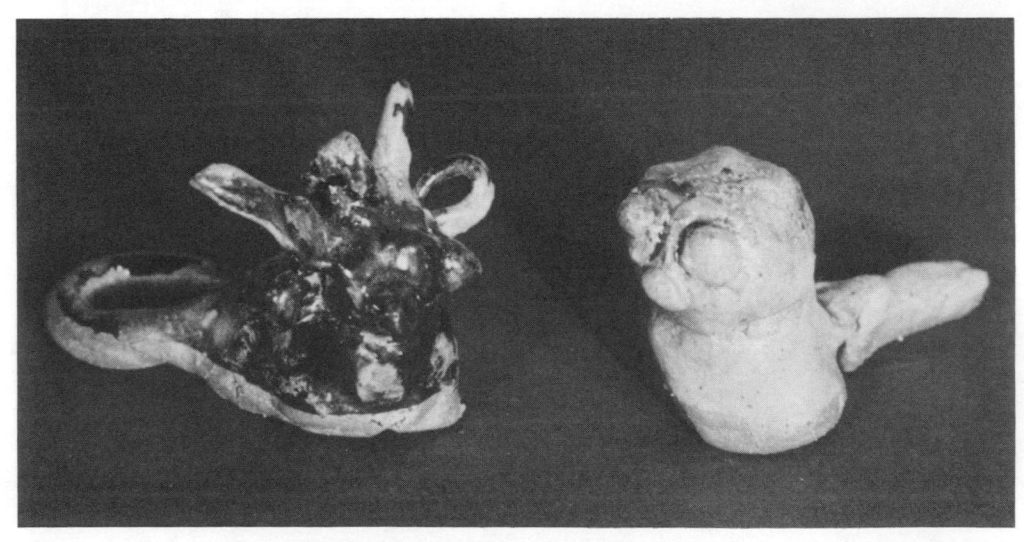

Left to right, by Nathan, age 5; and Greg, age 5

Clay: Modeling

MATERIALS
- Clay

OPTIONAL
- Sharp tools for scratching
- Tool for carving

1

Wedge or knead clay to soften and remove air bubbles.

2

Squeeze and press small piece of clay to make desired form . . .

3

or make form by attaching different sized balls and cylinders.

4

Roll out small coils to use as appendages or decorations.

5

Add bits of clay for features or details.

6

Clay forms may also be decorated by scratching designs in them with a sharp tool.

7

If clay pieces are too thick, they should be hollowed out inside to ¼″ thick if they are to be fired.

Activity 63 • Clay: Slab Work

Age Level: Preschool and up

Notes:

- For young children, slab work can be as simple as an imprinted clay tile, a class mobile or set of chimes, or a simple weed-pot plaque to hang on the wall.

- Older children can create more complex clay vessels out of slabs, such as boxes, vases, and bells.

- As with other projects involving clay, this work may be introduced again and again. There are endless possibilities for exploration and gaining technical skills.

Left to right, by Greg, age 5; anonymous

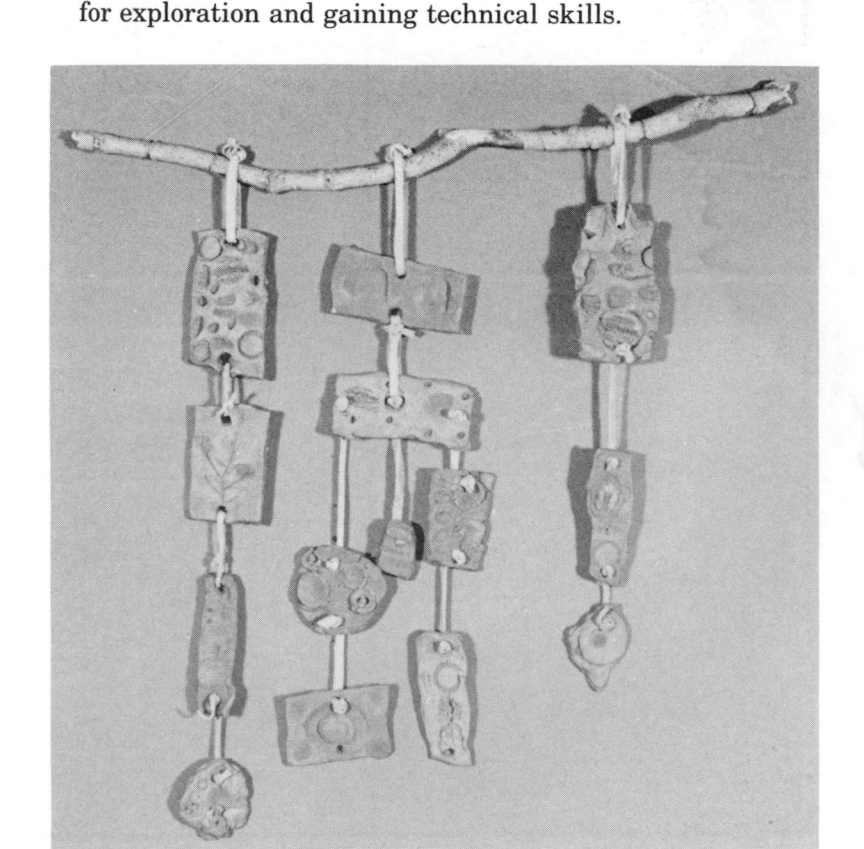

By students of The Children's Garden, a preschool

Clay: Slab Work

MATERIALS
- Clay
- Burlap
- Rolling pin
- Knife (to be used by older children only, under adult supervision)

OPTIONAL
- Objects for pressing,—acorns, hickory shells, rocks, sticks, shells, pinecones, string, etc.

1

Wedge or knead clay to soften and remove air bubbles.

2

Flatten by pressing or pounding with hands.

3

Sandwich clay between two pieces of burlap. Roll out clay evenly with rolling pin to about 1/4" thickness.

4

Remove clay from burlap. With knife cut out rectangular or square shapes.

5

Make vase by pinching two edges together with fingertips. Then add slab bottom.

6

Make a box out of five small slabs, smooth over creases with finger, adding more clay if necessary.

7

Make a tile hanging by pressing objects into clay tiles. Make two or more holes in each tile for threading string.

Activity 64 • Soapsuds Sculpture

Age Level: Preschool and up

Notes:

- This medium feels good to the touch and is malleable enough to create delicate interesting creatures.

- To extend this project, have children create a snow scene in which to place these creatures or try a three-dimensional forest.

- Do this project in conjunction with Activity 17, "Snow Painting." Have children snow-paint a two- or three-dimensional scene for their creatures to be arranged in, on, or around.

- Have children try snow painting on a box to create a home for their snow creatures.

- IMPORTANT: Warn preschoolers not to put soap in their mouths.

Counter-clockwise from left, by Matthew, age 4; Sarah, age 4; Matthew, age 4; and Kate, age 4

Soapsuds Sculpture

MATERIALS
- Large mixing bowl
- Measuring cup
- Tablespoon
- Soap powder
- Warm water
- Toothpicks
- Twigs, small stones, charcoal bits, acorn caps, etc.
- Electric beater (to be used *only* under adult supervision)

1
For approximately 1 cup of clay, pour ¾ cup of soap powder and 1 tablespoon warm water into mixing bowl.

2
Beat with electric beater to claylike consistency.

3
Press soap/clay mixture into balls, squeeze & mold into figures or shapes.

4
Use toothpicks to attach adjoining shapes.

5
Press decorations into figure if desired.

6
Allow to harden. This clay dries to a permanently hard finish.

7
Double, triple, or quadruple recipe to make larger quantities.

A wetter mixture can be used as imitation snow for decoration of pine boughs and Christmas trees.

Activity 65 • Wax Sculpture

Age Level: First grade and up

Notes:

- Here is the opportunity for children to actually "play" with this delectable material. Let children fully explore the properties and hardening time of wax before asking them to actually make a sculpture.

- Painting wax sculptures with melted crayon is an added sensory delight. (See Activity 18, "Encaustic.")

- Do this project in conjunction with other wax projects to give children a true understanding of wax and what it can do. (See Activity 18, "Encaustic"; Activity 27, "Paper Batik"; and Activity 28, "Batik.")

- IMPORTANT: Before attempting this project, read the precautions in Section One.

- CAUTION: Wax in the center of the cup can be quite hot and splatters easily. It should be carefully tested by an adult before the children are given the wax to work with. Children should *not* have free access to frypan.

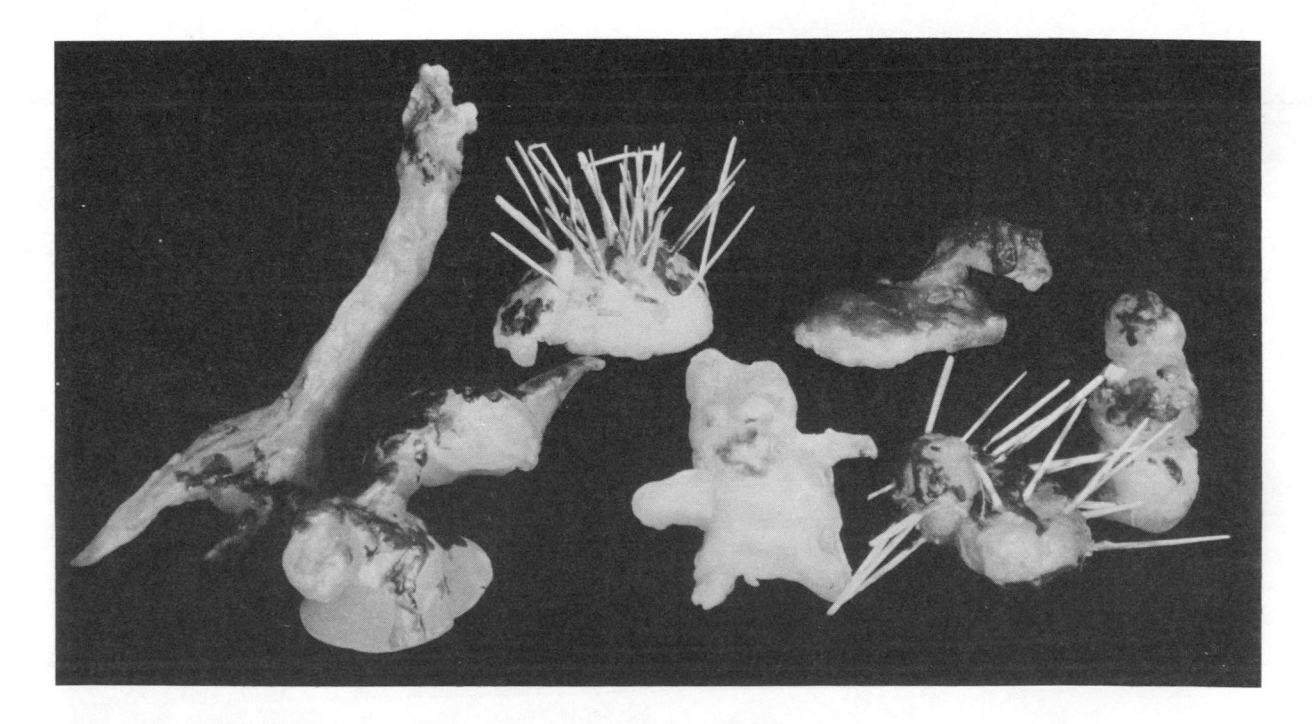

Top row, left to right, by Gina, age 4; Jen, age 4; Nathan, age 5; and Matthew, age 4; Bottom, from left to right by Robby, age 5; Heidi, age 4; and Jen, age 4

Wax Sculpture

MATERIALS
- Electric frypan or double boiler
- Paraffin wax
- Small paper cups
- Toothpicks

OPTIONAL
- Cupcake tin
- Crayons
- Cotton swabs
- Water

WARNING: Do not attempt this project without first reading all precautions on using hot wax.

1 Heat wax to melting (no hotter than 225° Fahrenheit). Scoop wax into paper cup and pour into other cups.

2 Let cups of wax stand until outer surface has begun to harden. Inside might be slightly liquid & can be tested by poking finger into center of cup. Make sure inside wax is cool enough to handle.

3 Peel paper cup away from wax form.

4 Over newspaper, squeeze, mold, twist, and stretch wax to make desired shapes.

5 Work swiftly as wax will harden in less than 5 minutes.

6 While wax is still warm, toothpicks can be stuck into it for decoration or used to hold shapes together.

7 Wax sculptures may be painted when hardened with melted crayon as directed in encaustic project. Small objects may be pressed into wax: buttons, stones, washers, etc.

Age Level: Preschool and up

Notes:

- Try this project in combination with other homemade sculpture materials, such as soapsuds or bread dough. (See Activities 64 and 67.) How are the sculptures alike? How are they different?

- This project could be tied into a discussion of sand. What is sand? How is it formed?

- If possible, take a trip to the beach and collect your own sand. Have adult boil the sand before using.

- Let the children play with cornstarch and water. Introduce it as a science experiment or as a textural experience.

Top row, left to right, by Nathan, age 5; Matthew, age 4.
Middle row Pippa, age 3; Matthew, age 5; Andrew, age 4.
Bottom row, left to right, by Nathan, age 5; and Andrew, age 4

Sand & Cornstarch Sculpture

MATERIALS
- Sand
- Cornstarch
- Water
- Alum
- Large pot
- Wooden spoon
- Measuring cup
- Measuring spoon
- Small objects, e.g., pinecone petals, twigs, cloves, apple seeds, toothpicks

CAUTION: Heating of the mixture should be done *only* by an adult.

1

Mix in pot:
  1 cup sand
  ½ cup cornstarch
  1 teasp. alum

2

Add ¾ cup hot water. Mix thoroughly.

3

Cook over medium heat until thick, stirring constantly.

4

When mixture has thickened, remove from heat and let cool. (Approx. 5–10 mins.)

5

Knead sand clay into balls and then shape into figures, animals, or abstract forms.

6

Press small objects into clay for texture, decoration, or as parts of animals—eyes, ears, quills, etc.

7

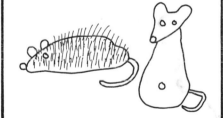

Let dry for a few days. This recipe makes about 2 cups of sand clay.

Activity 67 • Bread Dough Sculpture

Age Level: Preschool and up

Notes:

- When properly baked, these sculptures cook to a hard finish that can be varnished or painted with acrylic.

- Try making bread dough ornaments to decorate a holiday tree.

- Try making bread dough pottery.

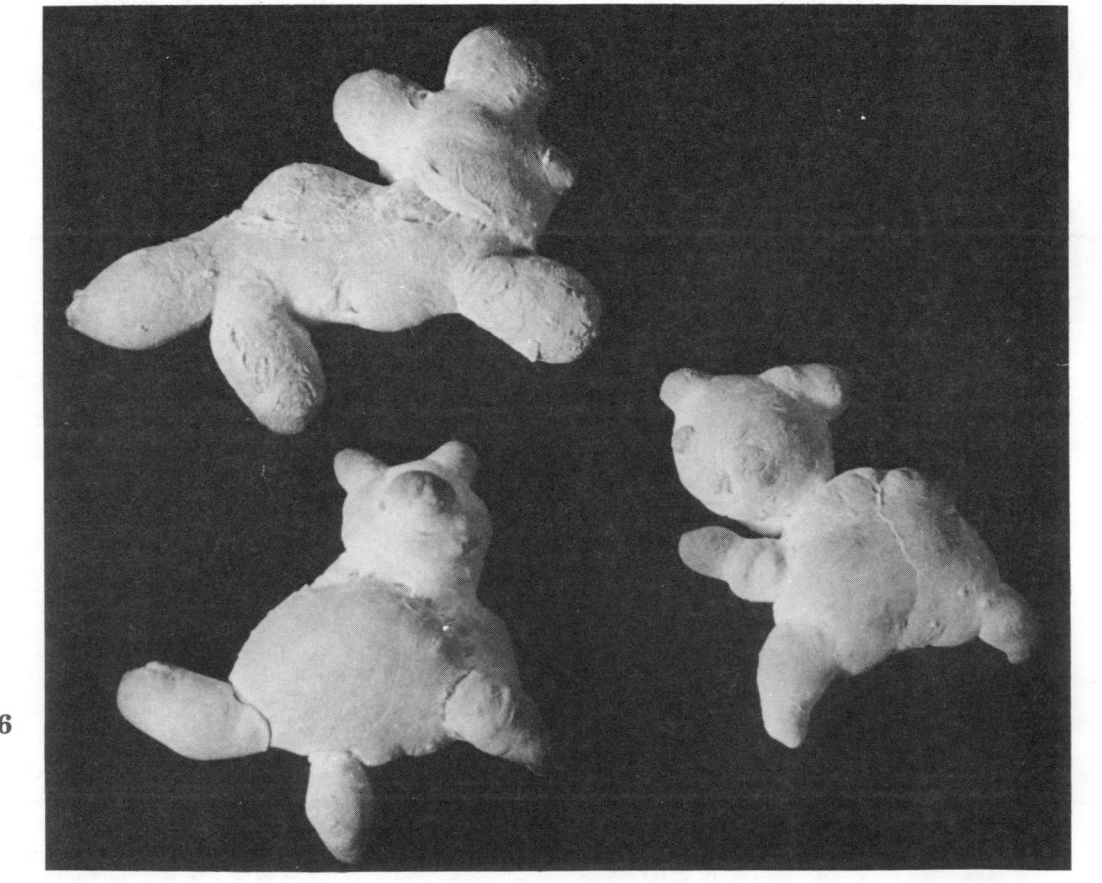

By Misa, age 6

Bread Dough Sculpture

MATERIALS
- Small and large mixing bowls
- Measuring cup
- Measuring spoons
- Large wooden spoon
- Egg beater
- Small clean dish towel
- Small pan
- Honey, water, yeast, egg white, salt, nonfat dry milk, corn oil, unsifted all-purpose white flour, cornstarch
- Watercolor brushes
- Cookie sheet

CAUTION: Beater to be used under adult supervision.

1

In a small bowl, mix 2 tbsp. honey, 1½ cups lukewarm water, 1 pkg. yeast. Let set for 2 minutes.

2

In large bowl, beat 2 egg whites with egg beater.

3

Add 1 tbsp. salt, ¾ cup nonfat dry milk, 1 tbsp. corn oil, yeast mixture. Then add 5–6 cups flour.

4

Knead.

5

Place in greased bowl and cover with towel. Let sit until doubled in size.

6

Punch down and model sculptures. Make forms fairly small because dough will rise in oven. Place them on an oiled cookie sheet.

7

Cook 2 tsp. cornstarch, ⅔ cup cold water, 1 tsp. salt until thick and clear. Brush mixture over dough. Bake sculptures at 450° for 10 mins., then 350° for 45–50 mins.

Activity 68 • Painted-Hand Puppet

Age Level: Preschool and up

Notes:

- Tempera paint seems to cover the skin better and create brighter colors, although as it dries it will begin to shrink and crack on the skin surface. Some children find this to be a strange sensation.

- Grease sticks do not cover as well, but leave the hand more flexible and comfortable. Keep cold cream handy to remove the grease stick paint.

- Try using acrylic paint for yet another effect.

- For a less messy approach, just paint features on the hand.

- Children may pair up and paint each other's hands.

- These puppets generally do not last long, so be prepared for a quick puppet show or "show and tell" immediately following this project!

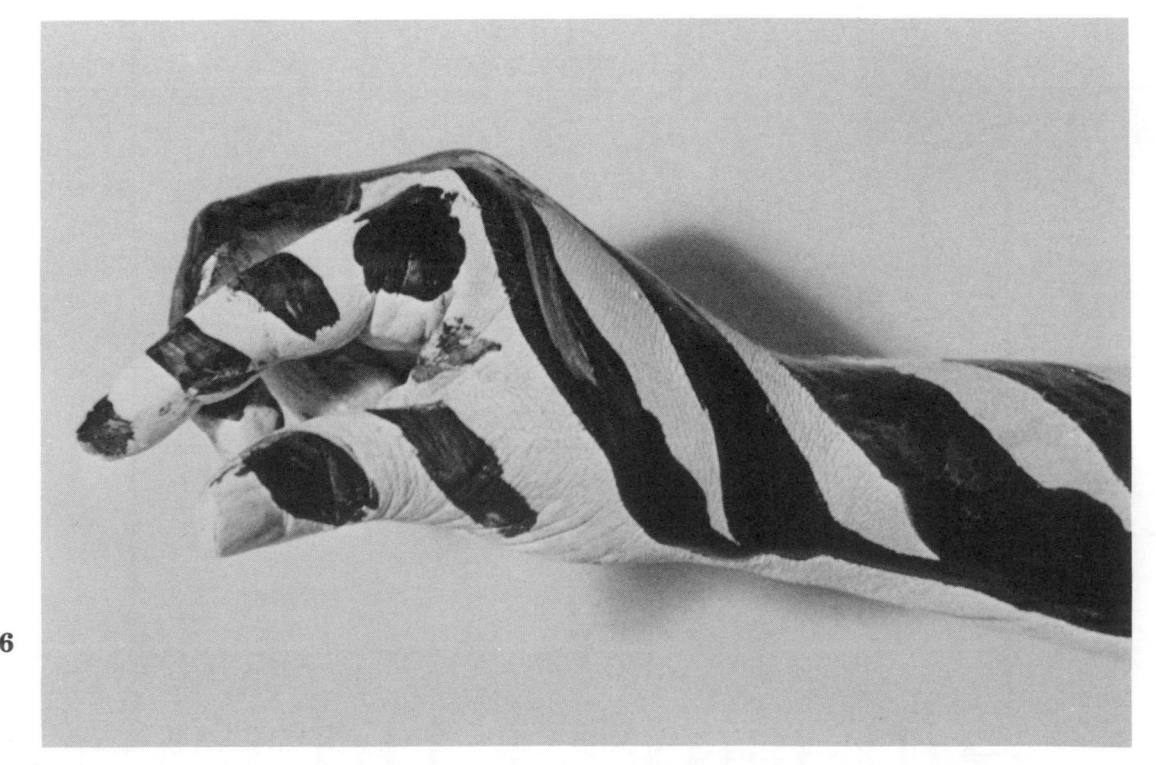

By Misa, age 6

Painted-Hand Puppet

MATERIALS
- Tempera paint
- Brushes
- Large plastic bowl
- Small plastic eyes
- Rubber cement glue
- Grease sticks (optional)
- Cold cream (optional)

1 Make several animal shapes with your hand. Choose one. With paint brush and tempera, color hand a base color.

2 Hand may be dipped into large bowl of paint for base color if preferred.

3 Shape hand into animal and paint on distinguishing features—stripes, spots, ears, nose, etc.

4 Eyes may be painted on . . .

5 or small plastic eyes may be glued on.

6 OPTIONAL: Grease sticks may be used instead of tempera paint.

7 Put on a puppet show with a friend!

Activity 69 • Stick Puppet

Age Level: Preschool and up

Notes:

- Children capable of drawing a rough figure are able to do this project. Younger preschoolers may want to simplify this project by drawing and/or decorating a simple face shape. Cloth may be stapled to the chin to create the body.

- Depending on the available scissors, children may need help cutting out the puppet shape.

- These puppets may be made in all shapes and sizes. A simple mural can be made to create a backdrop for a puppet show. Tables or desks lined up in front of the mural and draped with cloth can provide a stage for the puppet show.

Left to right, by Shannon, age 9; Emily, age 9

Stick Puppet

MATERIALS
- Oaktag or posterboard
- Pencil
- Markers
- Scissors
- ¼" wooden dowels
- Masking tape

OPTIONAL
- Felt scraps
- Wallpaper scraps
- Colored paper
- Yarn
- White glue
- Miscellaneous notions

1 With pencil, draw puppet figure on oaktag or posterboard.

2 Using markers, cut paper or wallpaper. Color and dress puppet.

3 Cut out puppet shape.

4 Tape wooden dowel to puppet back.

5 Puppets may also be dressed with felt or cloth scraps.

6 VARIATION: Animal shapes may be drawn and cut . . .

7 and decorated with cotton balls, fur scraps, etc.

165

Activity 70 • Paper Bag Puppet

Age Level: Preschool and up

Notes:

- This puppet is simple enough to be manageable by even the youngest of artists, yet can be elaborated upon so that it is challenging to older children as well.

- This puppet has a movable mouth and thus is particularly conducive to putting on puppet shows and storytelling.

- Try making extra large paper bag puppets using brown paper shopping bags.

Left to right, by Corinna, age 7; Holly, age 7

Paper Bag Puppet

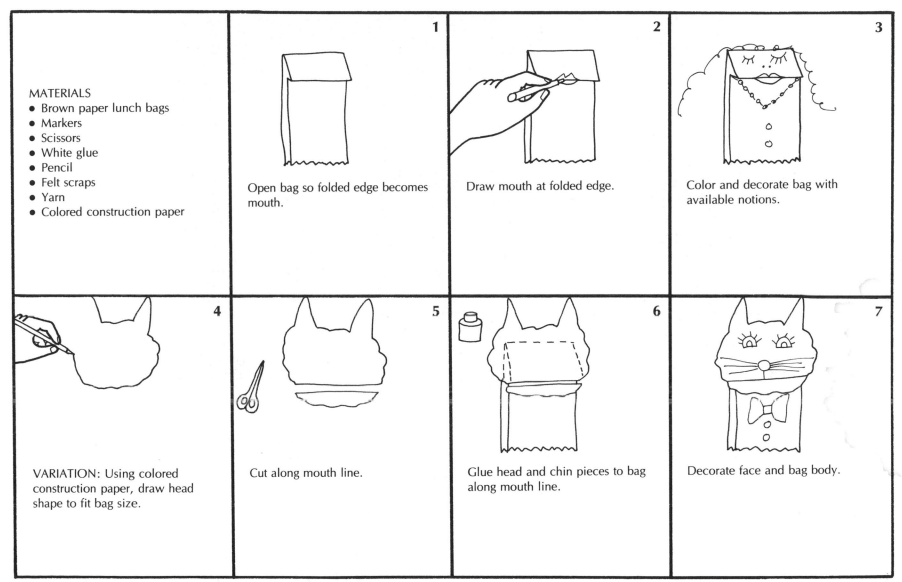

MATERIALS
- Brown paper lunch bags
- Markers
- Scissors
- White glue
- Pencil
- Felt scraps
- Yarn
- Colored construction paper

1 Open bag so folded edge becomes mouth.

2 Draw mouth at folded edge.

3 Color and decorate bag with available notions.

4 VARIATION: Using colored construction paper, draw head shape to fit bag size.

5 Cut along mouth line.

6 Glue head and chin pieces to bag along mouth line.

7 Decorate face and bag body.

167

Activity 71 • Spool Puppet

Age Level: Preschool and up

Notes:

- This project may be extended by having the class create a three-dimensional scene, such as a village, out of cardboard and small boxes and placing their spool puppets in the village. Children can also try a winter scene with cotton balls or Fiberfil® for snow and cut paper snowflakes hanging from above.

- Spool puppets may also be given wings and string to make a mobile. Add some Fiberfil® puffs for clouds.

Top left, by Matthew, age 4; bottom left, Gina, age 4. Top right by David, age 4. Bottom center by Samantha, age 3; bottom right by Kate, age 4

Spool Puppet

MATERIALS
- 6" cardboard conical spools, available at mills & recycle centers
- Cardboard toilet paper tubes
- Tempera paint in jars
- Brushes for tempera
- White glue in jars
- Brushes for glue
- Yarn
- Scissors
- Miscellaneous "bits"

1

Cut toilet paper tube in half and then punch hole with scissors into center of tube.

2

Place top of cone spool into hole to form head and body of puppet.

3

Paint puppet using several colors of tempera paint. Let dry.

4

Brush glue on top of head.

5

Then glue yarn in strands or bunches on top of the head.

6

Paint on facial features . . .

7

or glue on "bits" to make face. Also decorate cone body by gluing on "bits" such as buttons, washers, sequins, etc.

Activity 72 • Sock Puppet

Age Level: Preschool and up

Notes:

- This is one of the simplest puppets that can be easily managed and simply decorated by preschoolers. Older children can, of course, get into elaborate dressing and decorating if interesting scraps and notions are provided.

- Older children can sew on tails, ears, arms, and legs to create more elaborate creatures.

- Try using a variety of sock sizes ranging from very small to very large and create a whole "family" of sock puppets.

Left to right by Julie, age 6; Misa, age 6

Sock Puppet

MATERIALS
- Old socks
- Fiberfil® stuffing
- Toilet paper tubes
- Scissors
- Wide elastic bands
- White glue
- Felt scraps
- Cloth scraps
- Yarn
- Notions
- Yarn needle (optional)

1 Stuff toe of sock with Fiberfil®.

2 Insert one half of a toilet paper tube into stuffed head for neck.

3 Tightly fasten elastic band around tube at neck.

4 Cut felt shapes to make facial features . . .

5 and fasten with white glue.

6 Create hair and costume with yarn, cloth scraps, and notions.

7 Yarn hair could be sewed on instead, if desired.

Activity 73 • Paper Plate Puppet

Age Level: First grade and up; variation suitable for preschool and up

Notes:

- Paper plate puppets offer an easy way to make movable mouths and are particularly fun for children to use in puppet shows.

- These puppets, like others, can be easily embellished with interesting scraps and notions. Older children can make quite elaborate puppets using this basic paper plate model.

- Cloth sleeves can be simply made by gluing or stapling felt rectangles together. Older children may choose to sew cloth sleeves.

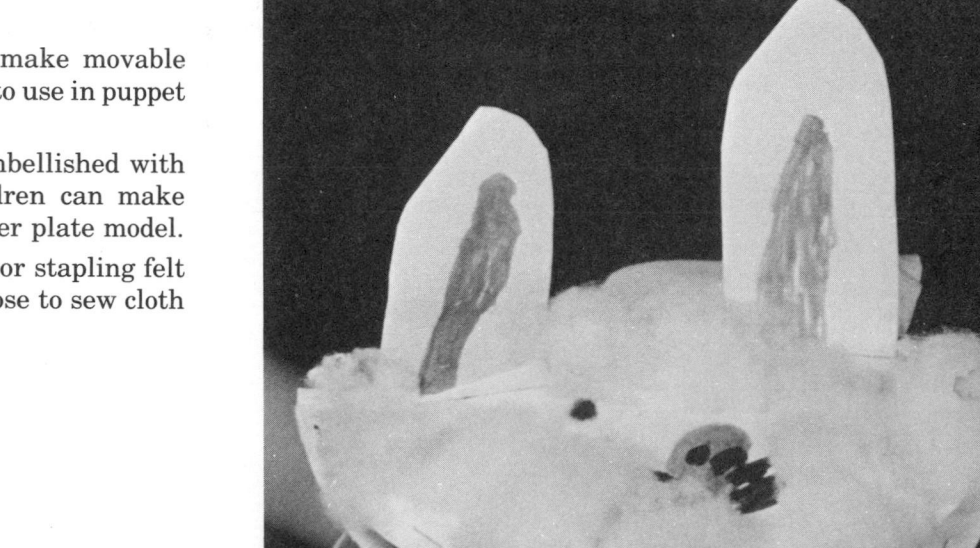

By Hillary, age 7

Paper Plate Puppet

MATERIALS
- Paper plates
- Stapler
- Scissors
- Markers
- Colored construction paper
- Felt scraps
- Cloth scraps
- Yarn
- White glue
- Needle and thread (optional)

1

Fold paper plate in half so that outer rim forms lips of puppet mouth.

2

Cut second paper plate in half. Glue or staple half plates onto upper and lower halves of folded plate to create pocket for fingers and thumb.

3

Sew or staple cloth or felt sleeve to plate, making sure not to close off finger pockets.

4

Decorate plate by gluing on eyes, nose, teeth, ears, hair, tongue, etc.

5

SIMPLER VARIATION: Staple paper plates along outside rim, right sides together.

6

Cut hole in back for puppeteer's finger.

7

Decorate plate with paint, markers, felt, paper scraps, yarn, etc. Drape cloth from plate for puppet body.

Activity 74 • Finger Puppet

Age Level: Preschool and up

Notes:

- Preschoolers can simply glue the felt tube with overlapping edges or can glue together identical puppet shapes. They will need help cutting felt shapes.

- Many interesting puppet creatures can be made by varying the puppet shape. Wide shapes or creatures with wings (for example, butterflies) work particularly well with young children as they can be easily glued.

- Try making a setting for the finger puppets by decorating the inside of cardboard boxes and cutting holes through the bottom for inserting fingers.

- Children might also decorate a plain butcher-style apron and turn themselves into the puppet backdrop!

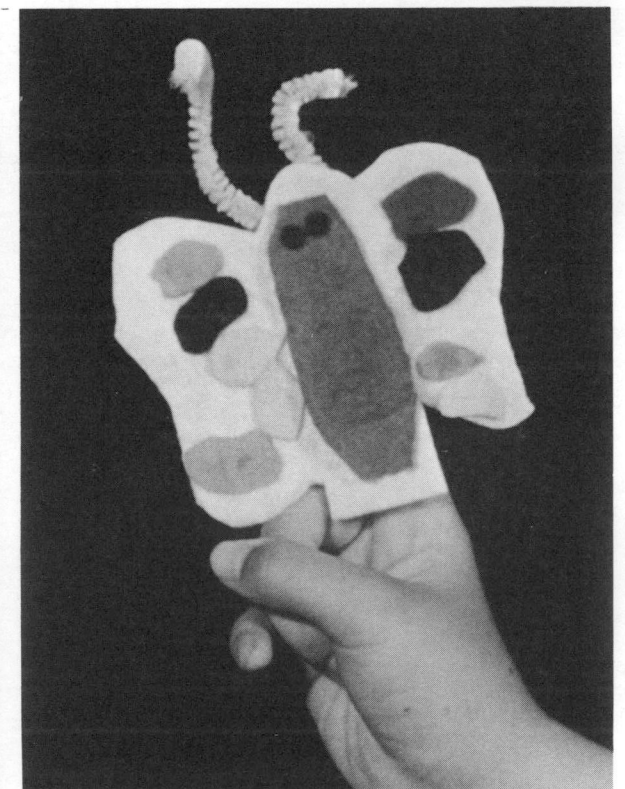

By Katy, age 8

By Julie, age 6

Finger Puppet

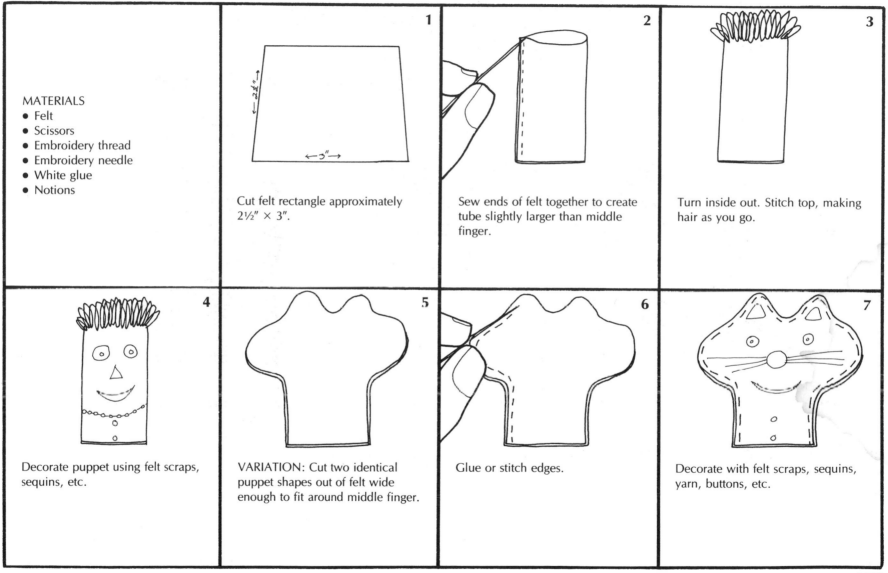

MATERIALS
- Felt
- Scissors
- Embroidery thread
- Embroidery needle
- White glue
- Notions

1 Cut felt rectangle approximately 2½" × 3".

2 Sew ends of felt together to create tube slightly larger than middle finger.

3 Turn inside out. Stitch top, making hair as you go.

4 Decorate puppet using felt scraps, sequins, etc.

5 VARIATION: Cut two identical puppet shapes out of felt wide enough to fit around middle finger.

6 Glue or stitch edges.

7 Decorate with felt scraps, sequins, yarn, buttons, etc.